Bangkok People

Bangkok People

James Eckardt

ASIA BOOKS

Published and Distributed by
Asia Books Co. Ltd.,
5 Sukhumvit Road Soi 61,
PO Box 40,
Bangkok 10110,
Thailand.
Tel: (662) 714 0740-2 ext. 221-223
Fax: (662) 381 1621, 391 2277

Typeset by COMSET Limited Partnership
Printed by Darnsutha Press Ltd.

ISBN 974-8237-35-4

Contents

Contents

Introduction

The only thing I like better than telling stories is listening to them. There are eight million stories in this naked city of Bangkok. Or nine. Or seven. No one knows for sure. Over the last seven years, I've been lucky enough to listen to thousands of Bangkok people, distilling their stories down to the cross-section collection of this book.

Businessmen, politicians, diplomats, movie stars, architects, builders, gem traders, boxers, go-go dancers, restaurant owners, hotel managers, street vendors, slum activists, yacht racers, fashion designers, taxi drivers, motorcycle taxi drivers, antique dealers, oil riggers, jazz musicians, labor leaders, catwalk models, slaughterhouse workers, doctors, textile tycoons, brewmasters, diamond cutters, silk dealers, tower crane operators, advertising executives, long distance truckers, army generals, computer wizards, drag queens and bungee jumpers—I interviewed them all. It was fun. People love to talk about their work.

All of these profiles first appeared in *Manager Magazine*, except for "Street Wise," *Bangkok Metro's* first cover story (then titled "Street Savvy"). *Manager*, Thailand's business and lifestyle monthly, was a great magazine. I joined as associate editor in June 1992, after 15 years on the beach in Songkhla. I came up to Bangkok as a wide-eyed yokel, speaking the Southern Thai dialect and knowing nothing, really, about this great sprawling rushing seething protean beast of a city.

When I first joined *Manager*, the 1992 elections were coming up and I interviewed such political heavyweights as Chavalit Yongchaiyudh, Surin Pitsuwan and Prachuab

Chaiyasan. They didn't faze me in the slightest. But I broke into a cold sweat when I was assigned an interview with Nanthida Kaewbuasai. She's my favorite singer ever. I've idolized her ever since she won her first talent show and I was petrified to meet her in person. I arrived an hour early for the interview and was squatting at the gate of her mansion like a beggar—a very nervous beggar—when Nathida's brother ambled by and invited me in.

Into the poolside pavilion where I waited miserably, rigid with stagefright, swept Nanthida. She took one look at me and asked, "What's wrong?"

"I'm scared."

She threw her head back and whooped with laughter. "Of *what*?"

We had two very giggly hours of talk, and afterward Nanthida said, "Jim, this wasn't like an interview. More like two friends chatting together."

I dined out on that comment for months. A year later, I ran into Nanthida at a rehearsal at the Queen Sirikit Convention Center. She gave me a warm welcome and looked me over. Life in the big city had added thirty pounds to my frame and turned my skin white.

"Jim, you've changed," she said solemnly.

"Yeah," I admitted, shamefaced. "I'm fat now."

"Nooo. You're more handsome than ever."

I'm *still* dining out on that remark.

Aside from Nanthida, the most important person I met in Bangkok was Peter Mittmann, someone I'd been dreaming of meeting since I first arrived in Thailand. Peter Mittmann is the brewmaster for Singha Beer. Reverently, I entered his office and approached the throne. I wanted to drop to my knees and kiss his hand. Peter, the soul of affability, put me at ease. He gave me a tour of the Boonrawd Brewery and afterward we retired to a private Bavarian tavern beside his office and sampled the day's brew. As a Serious Journalist, I had to plunge into the heart of my investigation of the beer industry. Peter helped me and together we demolished fourteen big bottles. It's a tough job being a journalist but somebody has to do it.

Of all the people I interviewed—from the highest reaches of society like Nanthida and Peter to the lowest depths like hookers and lawyers—no one has ever been rude to me. This is a Thai trait that even the harshest abrasions of Bangkok have failed to alter. People have been patient in the slow task of educating this dumb journalist, and quick with anecdotes and laughter. I want to thank them all.

Manager folded in July 1997, a victim of the Great Bust. During the hard times that followed, friends clothed my nakedness, gave food for my hunger and beer for my thirst. My thanks to Nate Thayer, Carol Bean, Michael Hayes, Collin Piprell, David Sutton, Ross Stevenson, Bill Page, Pat DeVito, Phil and Mui Blenkinsop, Duang Saengsawang, Brad Martin, Prangtip Daorueng, Santad Atthaseree, Carol Livingston, Colin Hastings, Greg and Gai Mollers, and my gimlet-eyed editor Richard Baker. John McDermott, Jonathan Taylor and the evil Blenkinsop contributed their images to this book. My groveling thanks to the three ace photographers and boon companions.

The Bust changed more lives than mine so I have appended a where-are-they-now epilogue about some of the people profiled here.

The Magus of Bangkok
The Magician—Dr. Penguin

Twenty-five years ago in Afghanistan, the Too Much Brothers—Dr. Himali and Count Bruno the Terrible—put on magic shows in dusty market squares. Top-hatted Dr. Himali would ask a villager to pick a card, any card. Count Bruno spreads out the deck on a table. Brandishing a dagger, Dr. Himali stabs a card from the fanned-out deck, and holds it up to a bemused villager. "Is this your card?" he asks.

"No."

"No? Um . . . is *this* your card?"

"No."

"*No?*"

In a blind fury, Dr. Himali jams the dagger down through the hand of Count Bruno who screams in pain. Dr. Himali snatches up the hand to reveal another card impaled on the bloody palm. "Is *this* your card?" he roars.

"*Yes!*"

The crowd goes wild.

○ ○ ○

"We were the bad boys of magic," Dr. Himali chuckles at the memory.

A decade later, in Thailand, Dr. Himali became Dr. Penguin, but let him tell the story. He starts in the middle:

"When I graduated from college in Santa Cruz, with a degree in magic, my girlfriend and I planned to travel for six months in Europe. The night before we left California, we were robbed at gunpoint in my apartment. We still had our air tickets, but we arrived at Heathrow Airport with all of 27

dollars. In London, I put on top hat and tails and did my magic act in the street. I collected 100 pounds.

"A few months later, in Zurich, I met up with a pair of German street clowns—Otto and Benelli—who'd been jailed in their own country. We were doing a show in a Zurich plaza and the police were after us again, but our audience locked arms and wouldn't let them through to arrest us. We brought the crowd into a beer hall and spent all the cash we'd collected—we were never interested in money—and even invited the police to join us. They refused, so we sent beers out to them.

"In Marrakech, at the huge Djma'a el Fna bazaar, it was like traveling back in time to medieval days: story-tellers, jugglers, acrobats, magicians, snake-charmers. I did magic with Berbers, Arabs and nomad Tuaregs. I was on Banana Beach in Morocco when a big red Mercedes fire engine drove up, and out fell a dozen long-haired freaks with bells in their beards. Their leader was a mime artist and one-man-band— an Austrian gypsy named Count Bruno the Terrible.

"We met up again in Goa and became the Too Much Brothers. By that time, I'd traveled overland from Istanbul, doing magic in village squares, staying in people's homes, and picking up a mini-circus of misfits—belly dancers, clowns, flame-swallowers and knife-throwers—along the way."

The Too Much Brothers were on the road for five years— in India, Sri Lanka, Afghanistan, Bhutan—but they spent the longest time in Nepal, where they learned the language, dressed as Nepali magicians, and played their own songs on a mandolin and a bamboo-and-coconut-shell violin. Their song, "Saili, Ra Maili Hong Kong Caye Chan," was a national hit. The lyrics tell of two unsuspecting travelers who are invited to dinner by a pair of female gold smugglers. The two girls slip out of the house, leaving the travelers to face the wrath of their father, who chases them all over Nepal seeking to cut off their noses.

Renamed "Wangchuk" and "Rinchin" in Nepali, the pair trekked slowly across the country, typically opening their shows at dawn under a village tree, just as the farmers were waking up. In Kathmandu, they became great favorites of the royal family, but their move into higher social circles did nothing to stem their anarchistic wit. At one hotel show they pulled the "shit trick" on the Russian ambassador. This burly dignitary had loudly proclaimed that he was not impressed by their magic, so they invited him on stage, sat him on a chair, dressed him up in a fright wig and clown nose, and passed balls and blew smoke through his ears.

"Suddenly the chair explodes!" the magician recalls with a laugh. "The Russian ambassador leaps up, frantically brushing his bottom, and there on the chair is a pile of shit. The look on his face brings the house down. I nonchalantly scoop up the shit and throw it out into the audience—where it magically turns into confetti. The crowd roared for ten minutes.

"We were invited to Sikkim by the *Karmapa*—the Buddhist Supreme Patriarch," he continues. "The *Karmapa* had a great sense of humor. He loved playing with our instruments, and honking our clown horns. There was a group of rich European pilgrims and they thought we were a sacrilege. During a show, one of the temple kids threw a *sampa*, a wheat ball, at a big Finnish guy. He thought I'd done it and came charging at me, ready to kill. The *Karmapa* cooled him down with a water hose."

In Bhutan, they met Prince Bhirabhongse Bhanudej, the race car champion. "Prince Bhira invited us to Thailand in 1978. I fell in love with the country, and for a year we traveled all over—from Phuket to Nong Khai—giving shows in *wats,* schools and orphanages. After another couple of years in Nepal and Bhutan, we turned up in Singapore in 1981."

Singapore was not quite ready for the Too Much Brothers. Police arrested them for not having a work permit, but soon they were performing on television and at company functions in luxury hotels. They took over a 100-year-old house on Pasar Panjang Hill—supposedly haunted by a Chinese monk—and quickly fell to terrorizing their guests through secret passageways, trap doors, exploding refrigerators, talking toilet seats, and soap that lathered into blood. They would warn house guests to be sure to close their windows at night to keep out Singapore's famous flying rats, but of course, the bedroom window was nailed open and as soon as the worried guest climbed into bed, a rocket balloon would shriek into the room. "People were *spooked*!" Dr. Penguin remembers with satisfaction. "They fled that house in terror."

Wangchuk/Dr. Himali was reincarnated as Dr. Penguin when he took his Japanese girlfriend on a motorcycle trip up to Phuket. On his way to perform at a temple fair, he was caught out in the rain, and as he waddled across a muddy field, spectators laughed and called out, "*Nok* penguin! *Nok* penguin!" A new star was born.

The Too Much Brothers traveled on to Bali and then to Los Angeles, where they stayed at the home of actor, James Coburn, whom they had befriended in Nepal. They appeared on the Johnny Carson Show. At a club in Fort Worth, Texas, they played their Nepali-Gypsy-Thai-Chinese-Malay music and jammed with jazz musician, Ornette Coleman. They were slated to appear on *Saturday Night Live,* but a week before, at a benefit concert for Tibetan refugees on a ranch in New Mexico, a weird and terrible tragedy struck.

An abandoned refrigerator, stuffed with dynamite, had been standing out in the desert sun for years. Somehow it exploded, taking off Count Bruno's right leg. Six years of court battles followed before he was awarded compensation. Suspicious of the judge, Dr. Penguin was thrown out of the courtroom for sporting a lapel button with the message, "*Why Hire a Lawyer When You Can Buy a Judge?*" Retired from show business, Count Bruno now lives in Germany.

Back in Singapore, Dr. Penguin did magic shows at Jurong Bird Park and Singapore Zoo, which led to a weekly TV program called, "What's New at the Zoo?" and a comedy radio series, "Dr. Penguin's Magic Children's Show." He married his girlfriend Kyoto, a well-known journalist, and was soon the father of baby daughter, Tashi.

Was the Doctor turning respectable?

Not according to the Singaporean police.

Though supported by the local Arts Council and the Tourist Bureau, Dr. Penguin had to fight in court for the rights of visiting performers to the 1987 Singapore Arts Festival. The police required that visiting troupes depart immediately after their performances, and also demanded advance scripts for every act—including the Royal Canadian Mime Troupe.

Dr. Penguin won his case, but his troubles had only begun. Hosting a clown and magic show at the open-air Piranha Club on Orchard Road, the Doctor was confronted by police claiming that the clown shows were too loud. The fine was S$2,000. The next night, the club staged a musical show. Police slapped them with another S$2,000 fine: the band was too loud. The third night was a mime show. Another S$2,000 fine: the audience was laughing too loud.

Finally, Dr. Penguin stepped over the line. At a stand-up comedy club, he told a political joke about Prime Minister Lee Kuan Yew.

"A delegation from the ruling PAP (People's Action Party) told me I had 24 hours to get out of the country," Dr. Penguin recalls. "No charges were filed, and much later, there was some sort of apology. But I took them seriously enough to pack up my car and drive across the causeway with Kyoto and Tashi. We wound up in Phuket, but there wasn't much work there, so we flew on to Hong Kong."

In the colony, Dr. Penguin wandered amid the posh Duddell's restaurant appearing to smash Rolex watches and burn holes in Armani shirts. Michael Jackson was supposed to visit Duddell's after a concert in Tokyo, but his security chief was worried. If there was a mob of press waiting for him at Kai Tak Airport, Michael Jackson swore he would get right back on the plane.

"I told the security chief, 'Leave it to me,'" Dr. Penguin recalls with an evil gleam in his eye. "I grabbed Peggy Johnson—a black Canadian singer—and took her up to my apartment, where Kyoto and I dressed her up as Michael Jackson, complete with black slouch hat.

We drove off to the airport. The arrival lounge was packed with photographers and suddenly I shout, 'MICHAEL, WHERE'S THE LIMO? QUICK, MICHAEL! RUN! TAXI! TAXI!' We jump into a cab and the press mob is all around us, pounding on the windows and pulling at the doors. 'Michael's never coming back to Hong Kong!' I yelled at them. We took off on a high-speed car chase and lost them downtown. Minutes later, the real Michael Jackson arrived to an empty airport.

"I broke the hoax the next day to a reporter friend at the *South China Morning Post*. A rival newspaper claimed I was an impostor with no connection to Michael Jackson, but the next day, the *Post* ran a big photo of me grinning behind him on the Ocean Park roller-coaster. We had a ball."

But there was not much work in Hong Kong either—"A small town, really," the Doctor says—and with an infant son in tow, the family moved to Bangkok in 1988.

Dr. Penguin became the official magician at the Oriental Hotel, and performed three daily shows at Safari World. On behalf of Safari World, he traveled to Papua New Guinea to recruit a 22-member dance troupe.

"For three months, wandering from island to island—New Britain, New Ireland, the Trobriands—it was just like the old days, doing shows in schools and villages," Dr. Penguin remembers fondly. "You walk for three hours over a mountain range and you're back 10,000 years. Those people took their magic seriously. I pulled a 100 *kina* note out of one guy's ear and his friends jumped all over him trying to pull money out of his other ear."

Back in Bangkok, Dr. Penguin opened the state-of-the-art Imagica Show at The Mall 6's open-air arena. He hosted the "Dr. Penguin Radio Show," and six hours of comedy on Sundays—"The Magic Mystery Tour." During the May events of 1992, he stayed on the air—despite the NPKC junta's broadcast censors—playing topical favorites like "A Boy Named Sue," "Hit the Road, Jack," "Power to the People," and "Take the Money and Run."

Dr. Penguin has also been on trips to perform in Laos, Zimbabwe and, most recently, Australia. In Sydney, magician friends took him to a club to meet a famous stripper named Veronica. The next night, he returned to her club. "I fanned out a deck of cards and said, 'Veronica, last night I dreamed you picked a card and I wrote your name on it, but now I can't remember which card it was. Do you remember?' She picked the two of diamonds and, of course, her name was written across it. She loved that trick. She gave me a signed poster of herself in return."

The poster is the newest of many treasures in Dr. Penguin's Bangkok apartment. There are ancestor spirit masks from Papua New Guinea, Sarawak, Zimbabwe, Sri Lanka; thighbone whistles and an ancient magic wand from Tibet; bookshelves of classic magic texts by Thomas Nelson Downs, Dai Vernon, Henry Hay and Hoffmann; professional magician magazines like *Genii, Tops, Magic* and *Tannin's Magic Manuscript*; esoteria like an Indian pamphlet entitled *How to Pick a Pocket*; and a trunkload of props including pulls, false thumbs, explosive devices, hoops, cups-and-balls, collapsing ketchup bottles, disappearing spiders, and a rubber chicken named Ute.

"All magicians are crazy about collecting," Dr. Penguin comments. "As their wives will tell you." He holds up a pair of red, foam rubber balls. "This is a favorite of Stevie Wonder. I showed him this when we did a show in Taiwan."

He puts the balls in my hands and says, "Now squeeze. Turn your hands over and open them up. Still one ball in each palm, right? But one's *heavier*, do you feel it?"

He squeezes my two hands shut and turns them over again. "Okay, now open them."

I open my hands and one palm is empty. From the other pops two red balls.

Dr. Penguin does have a real name. He was born Chedly Saheb-Ettaba, forty-odd years ago, in Tangier. His father was a Moroccan linguist and his mother an American writer, part of an expatriate circle that included Paul Bowles and William Burroughs. When he was six, his father died and he returned to the US with his mother. Two years later, he was accepted into St. Paul's Cathedral Choir in London. Along with schoolboy pranks, he took up the study of magic. A close family friend was the famous comic magician, Tommy Cooper.

"On my eleventh birthday, I put on a magic show. Uncle Tommy was drunk. 'You stink,' he told me. 'You have to get out on the street if you want to do magic.' So I did. I was gone three weeks before the police caught me doing a show in front of Lincoln Cathedral."

At 13, he rejoined his mother in San Francisco, but he hated American high school. The schoolboy pranks grew more outrageous, and the study of magic more serious. He was practicing card tricks four and five hours a night. San Francisco was the place to be for a magician. It was the home of the great masters, Dai Vernon and Charlie Miller. Young Chedley hung out in magic stores, made his debut at the Magic Cellar Club, and performed on the plazas of Ghiridelli Square and the Cannery.

"Out in the street, the audience surrounds you on all sides and you *have* to be excellent," Dr. Penguin says. "Established nightclub magicians despised us long-haired freaks, but in time, they recognized our artistry. We were doing magic for love of the art, not for money. And you're always learning. The older you get, the better you get. The art goes all the way back to ancient Egypt. At the King Tutankhamoun exhibit, I saw magic tools we still use today—except these were made of gold.

"Magic is a definition for what we don't understand. *Deja vu* is real. We just don't know how to describe it by the normal laws of physics. In my travels I saw spirit possession and exorcism—the *Wassadessa* devil dancers of Sri Lanka, for example. There's much more out there than can be understood by science."

But the Doctor soon veers off this serious vein and launches into another prank anecdote. "In Kathmandu, Count Bruno fell off his motorcycle and was in the hospital under sedation. So I went down to Meat Street and bought up all these livers and kidneys and intestines. Then I put on a white coat and snuck into the hospital. . . ."

The Making of an MP

The Candidate—Orathai Karnchanachusak

June 22nd:

Dressed in a school uniform, Orathai Karnchanachusak could easily pass for a university student. Instead, she is addressing an auditorium of 800 Chulalongkorn undergrads, urging them to turn out to vote her into parliament.

"I'm a Chula graduate myself, 28 years old, and I stand for a new generation of politicians," Orathai tells the students. "I need your help in this election."

In 11 days, voters in her Bangkok Constituency 2—Bangrak, Pathumwan, Phra Nakhon, Samphan Thawong and Pom Prap—will go to the polls. Palang Dhama candidate Orathai is running 15 points behind Murat Bunnag, veteran Democrat MP and House Speaker. If she is daunted by the odds, she does not show it. She is calm, poised and relaxed, with a resonant speaking voice.

In an interview outside the auditorium, Orathai explains that she registered with the Palang Dhama party in 1992. "I was attracted by their honesty, their competence, and their concern for poor people who've been left out of the country's development."

After winning a municipal council seat 18 months ago, she was picked by party leader Taksin Shinawatra to run on his ticket in Constituency 2. The area includes Yaowarat — Chinatown—where Orathai's family has long been prominent. Her Chinese immigrant grandfather made his fortune in tapioca trading; her father, Song, is a famous boxing promoter of champions in both Thai and international arenas. Orathai naturally followed into the family business before

jumping into politics. Relatives and neighbors form the bulk of her twenty-something campaign staff.

From Chulalongkorn, Orathai races to City Hall on the pillion of a motorcycle ridden by campaign aide, Wanchai Kiatchaiyawuth. The motorcycle is rigged up with a loud-speaker, and clutching a microphone, Orathai broadcasts a rolling speech about the horrors of Bangkok traffic and her party's determination to crack the problem. People on the sidewalk grin and wave.

In the parking lot of City Hall, Orathai meets up with running mate Suranand Vejjajiva; party founder, Chamlong Srimuang; and a dozen placard-bearing volunteers who form a flying picket line as Chamlong plunges past a row of shops and into a warren of slum alleyways. Here is where the votes are. An old hand at shoe-leather politics, Chamlong sets a blistering pace. Orathai and Suranand scurry to keep up. Introducing themselves to people in their shops and homes, they *wai* and ask voters to pull the levers for numbers four, five and six (Taksin, Orathai and Suranand). Orathai leaves behind a trail of admiring comments: "She's so young!" "She's so cute!" "She's so tiny!"

In one courtyard, Chamlong addresses an impromptu crowd through a bullhorn, making the pitch for a new generation to tackle the traffic and economy problems. He jokes that the only qualification Orathai lacks is height (she's barely five foot).

They canvass cafes, noodle shops, gas stations, and a giant outdoor market. Orathai lingers to talk to vendors, then sprints to catch up to Chamlong, windmilling her arms like a boxer. They race door to door through wooden slums tucked behind temple walls, and then break out into the wide spaces of Rajadamnern Road. Orathai puts her arm around a wilting teenage volunteer.

"I've lost five kilos so far," Orathai confides, swigging water like a marathon runner. "We've been campaigning for nearly a month. I'm lucky to get four hours of sleep a night. Our rivals are out in the street too, but I don't think for as long and as hard as we are."

After three hours, they are on Khao San Road, being greeted ecstatically by Indian tailors and coffee shop waitresses. An aging American hippie leaps to his feet to shake Chamlong's hand. "I seen you in the papers, man!" he cries. "You're too good!"

"You're too bad," Chamlong smiles back. The freaks in the coffee shop stand and applaud.

Down Chakraband Road to New World Department Store, the pavement is thronged with shoppers. Orathai and Suranand dash in and out of stores, and Chamlong introduces them to sidewalk crowds. Around a corner, they come upon a school van packed with children in uniform. Orathai gives them all hugs. "Tell your parents to vote for Uncle Chamlong's party," she laughs. "Remember numbers four, five, six. What are those numbers?"

"Four, five, six!" they chorus gleefully.

June 27th:

At 7:30 a.m., Orathai and Suranand meet at Suan Lum Market and begin working the Pathumwan district. They linger longer with family groups in this unfamiliar neighborhood of grimy machine shops and low, wood shophouses. Wanchai, on his motorcycle, is the advance man, looking like a fighter pilot with headphones over his helmet. Orathai's sister, Nui, and her secretary, Wan, lead volunteers in passing out party pamphlets. At 1:30, they break for a hurried lunch of *khao man gai*. Sifting through a stack of newspapers, the candidates are cheerful, but show signs of strain. Orathai's eyes are heavy-lidded and her voice is slightly hoarse; Suranand's features are drawn.

A friend picks up Orathai for her next appointment, a talk at the Debsirin High School. "The kids can't vote but their parents can," she explains, stretching out in the front seat of the car.

"How many hours did you sleep last night?"

"Three."

"What will you do after the election?"

"There's no plan for a vacation. We have a lot of business to take care of. But I do hope for some time to sleep."

At Debsirin School's closed-circuit TV studio, Orathai gives an extemporaneous talk on education that is broadcast to 4,600 students in 100 classrooms. She takes softball questions from a half dozen students and concludes with a pep talk on the elections. "Talk to your parents. You are responsible for your government too, even if you can't vote."

Afterward, she is mobbed in the corridor by students, poses for photos with teachers, and escapes on the motorcycle with Wanchai. Next stop is Chula Apartments—a low-income public housing project. Four bare-concrete blocks, five stories tall, house 770 families, and all but seventy are registered to vote. The Democrat and Nam Thai candidates have already been through here, leaving behind their wall stickers. As Orathai and Suranand climb to the top floor and work their way down from flat to flat, their reception is less than rapturous. This portion of the over-proselytized urban poor appears jaded by politicians. A group of guitar players stare back with blank faces as Orathai makes her pitch. Only one returns her *wai*.

"This is better than the Klong Toey projects last night," comments Orathai's sister, Nui. "There are five buildings, *twelve* stories tall, and of course the elevators don't work."

The team breaks for dinner, then heads to Yaowarat to work the shopping crowds. Orathai will get four hours sleep tonight.

June 28th:

At 6:30 a.m., Orathai and Suranand meet up with Taksin Shinawatra to canvass the huge Chulalongkorn Medical Center. A hyper-voluble nursing instructor leads Taksin into a cavernous cafeteria, where he dutifully hands out election cards to nurses and doctors coming off duty. Stiff in public, Taksin lacks the running patter and charisma of Chamlong. Orathai lags behind to work the cafeteria tables, chatting with hospital staff and visitors.

An hour later, Taksin departs in his BMW limo. Orathai and Suranand stay to talk and *wai* their way up seven floors of the hospital. The ranked chairs in the waiting areas serve as a perfect theater for Orathai to stand and introduce herself to patients. At 8:30, she is on her way home to the family complex at Thanon Song Wat. In the office of her father's tapioca company, she eats breakfast with her inner circle and city councilman, Adul Laohaveranit. The latest newspaper polls show her running four points ahead of Marut Bunnag. "I don't believe in polls," Adul tells Orathai. "But from what I can see on the street, you're looking good."

Behind the office, huge warehouses of tapioca lead down to the Chao Praya and a riverside boxing camp. A shophouse serves as Orathai's campaign office, where a half dozen burly boxers are busy folding pamphlets. At 10 a.m., the team— Orathai, Suranand, Adul, Wanchai, Wan, Nui and a dozen teenage volunteers—are ready to hit the streets again. "We'll be moving fast today," Orathai says. "This is my own neighborhood."

With Orathai in the lead, they move at a brisk clip down riverside streets lined with tiny offices in front of warehouses stacked with rice, peanuts, peppers, garlic and cooking oil. People leap up from behind their desks to greet her with smiles and hugs. Orathai is definitely the favorite daughter. She is Jack Kennedy in a Boston Irish ward.

They turn down Thanon Rachawong in the heart of Yaowarat. Orathai enters the local Bangkok Bank and makes a short speech. Bank tellers stand up and applaud. Crossing the street again, Orathai hands out pamphlets to motorcycle riders, bus passengers, and a bemused traffic cop. They work the back alleys down to the river again, through warrens of tiny, wooden, 100-year-old Chinese shophouses. Ancestor shrines glow red in each house. Ornate spirit houses overlook the river. To the elderly immigrants, Orathai says numbers four, five and six in Chinese.

At 12:30 p.m., the volunteers break for *kway tiao,* but Orathai, Suranand and Adul make one more turn around a block of porcelain vendors before devouring a quick lunch. They hop in a van and are whisked off to the Pan Pacific Hotel on Rama IV Road. From century-old slums, they are suddenly in the rooftop garden of Bangkok's newest luxury hotel, where Taksin is hosting a lunch for business tycoons. Orathai is a star here too. Men and women crane their necks to catch a glimpse of her as she *wai*s from table to table. She gives a quick speech on her usual theme of a new generation in politics, and is off again on Wanchai's motorcycle, tearing through the lunch hour traffic to meet Chamlong at Yaowarat's Old Siam Shopping Center.

They set off at a gallop past the cloth shops of Burapa Road. Shopkeepers lean forward on counters, ready to greet the rolling show. Chamlong darts down a narrow alley and suddenly they are in India. Here the shops sell Indian spices, incense, clothing, videos and cassettes. Indians are packed tightly in hole-in-the-wall tea shops. The alley debouches into a huge open-air market where Chamlong gathers a crowd to introduce Orathai. "She's 28 years old. She's not a kid. She's a candidate. She's number five, Suranand's number six. I don't have a number. I'm zero."

Shopgirls stop Chamlong to swap jasmine wrist garlands for Palang Dhama caps. As two women and a child squeeze past them down a narrow aisle, Chamlong gestures to Orathai to cut them off. "Two votes there. Two and a half."

Three hours later, the show comes to a halt at the Grand China Hotel and Business Center. Chamlong leaves, and the team breaks for dinner. Orathai and Nui take the elevator to the 15th floor and the Palang Dhama's strategy room. There are ranks of computers and wall maps with colored pins. Two statisticians assure Orathai that both she and Suranand stand a good chance to win the election, four days away.

At 6:30 a.m. the next morning, Taksin, Orathai and Suranand will meet at Lumpini Park for a last motorized blitz of the district. They will walk through Bangrak for six hours, and Phra Nakhon for another six. The next night, a final Palang Dhama rally will attract 10,000 people to a mud-soaked Sanam Luang.

July 2nd:

Election Day. The polls have been closed for an hour. The lobby of Palang Dhama headquarters on Ramkamhaeng's Soi 39 is packed with supporters watching the ongoing results on TV. Camera crews are interviewing Taksin, who is flanked by Orathai and Suranand. Upstairs in party offices, Nui is working the phones to track the latest figures. At 5:10 p.m., Taksin and Democrat Supachai Panitpakdi have a lock on first and second places. Orathai trails Marut Bunnag by 300 votes in a close battle for the district's third seat. Over the next 15 minutes, Orathai surges ahead by 99 votes, then by 344. The narrow upset brings the camera crews running. Smiling serenely, Orathai tells Channel 9 that the outcome is still uncertain, but she is grateful that so many voters have put their trust in her. A female supporter breaks down in tears of joy. Orathai hugs her and photographers stampede for the picture.

By 5:30, Orathai's lead has shrunk to 12. Ten minutes later, Marut is up by 518 votes. Smile still in place, Orathai gives another cool, self-possessed interview to Channel 7. At 6:04, with 99% of the vote counted (45,489 to 45,366), TV commentators give the election to Marut by 123 votes. "There'll be a protest and a recount," Suranand says grimly. The pack of photographers rushes for the stairs at a rumor that Orathai is down in the lobby, crying. "No, she's not," snaps a journalist. "She's in a conference room up here. I just saw her and she's smiling. She's laughing."

Nui stays on the phone, checking late results from Pom Prap district. At 8 p.m. she begins to calculate that Orathai has won; by 11 p.m., she is sure. The final official tally is 45,542 to 45,451. Orathai wins by 91 votes. She has bucked the odds all the way. Of the 391 newly-elected MPs, she is of the 6.5% who are female, and the 1.3% under thirty years old.

July 11th:

Following a hectic week of thanking her supporters, plotting strategy at Palang Dhama headquarters, being interviewed on TV talk shows, and attending Parliament for her swearing-in ceremony, MP Orathai Karnchanachusak relaxes at her home on Song Wat Road. She attributes her winning campaign to the stamina of her election team. "I took it day by day," she comments. "I was exhausted, but knew it would end soon. I had a strong determination to win."

As a new MP, entitled to a 15 million baht development fund, she intends to create parks in her overcrowded district. "I'll also be funding educational media—TVs, sound labs, computers—as well as sports equipment for the district's schools. I got a very good response in the schools. My hope is that this new generation will become more involved in politics."

Of Patpong Road, which is in her district, she comments, "No one with an education or job opportunities works on Patpong. Of women's rights in general, we 24 female MPs should band together to push bills that promote equality. There are still very few women in politics because they see it as a dirty game played by men.

The day after her election, 100 Democrat supporters marched to City Hall in protest. They claimed that the presence of five Orathai campaign workers and two city councilmen at the Pom Prap District Hall late Sunday night had something to do with her narrow win there.

"My supporters were just there to check on the vote count," Orathai explains. "I saw the protesters the next day at City Hall. They looked so angry I was afraid to get out of the car. A lot of people bet against me in this campaign."

Fight Night

The Muay Thai *Boxers*

"Camp" seems a strange word to describe the warren of rooms stuck down a narrow alley off Bangkok's Central Hospital, but this is indeed the Chu Wattana Boxing Camp. The air is thick with the smell of liniment and the sounds of training: grunts, explosive breaths, the thwack of gloves against punching bags.

In a cramped area partly open to the sky, fighters are pounding and kicking the hell out of five sand-filled body bags. Sparring partners are squared off on the floor, practicing clinches and throws, while other boxers send a rain of flying fists and feet at trainers armored like gladiators in leather helmets, breastplates, greaves, thick arm shields.

In one corner, Nophodej Rewadee—known as "The Lion of Singburi"—is shadow-boxing before a full-length mirror. In five days' time, at Rajadamnern Stadium, he is going up against the country's most popular *Muay Thai* fighter, Wanwisit Kannorasingh. The two featherweights (122–126 lbs) have met before. Nophodej won once; Wanwiset, four times. Nophodej is going into the fight a 5–4 underdog.

Nophodej climbs up into the ring now for a four-round workout with his trainer. Soon both are drenched with sweat as Nophodej finds his rhythm, rocketing a dazzlingly fast barrage of kicks—whackwhackwhack!—against his mentor's hips, ribs and stomach. "*Heeah, heeah, heeah*," he grunts as he lands each blow. "Whoosh! *Heeah, heeah!*"

"Nophodej's strength is his kicking power, especially to the body," comments Chujaroen Raweearamwongse, camp manager and promoter of the upcoming fight. "Wanwisit's advantage is tremendous eye-hand coordination, good elbow

work, and speed. Nophodej will train hard for the next two days, then switch to light exercise for the last two days before the fight.

"The training schedule here is always the same, seven days a week. The twenty boxers get up at five-thirty, run for an hour, and then jump rope and practice on the bags till breakfast—heavy on milk and eggs—at nine-thirty. They rest till three in the afternoon and then it's another round of rope-skipping, bag and sparring practice till dinner at six. Afterward they're free to watch television or boxing videos. At ten, they go upstairs to the dorm and sleep."

The cramped spartan conditions (the kitchen is squeezed in next to the boxing ring) and the monastic discipline have produced a steady succession of champions, whose names Chujaroen proudly ticks off on his fingers.

After a ferocious workout, Nophodej's trim muscular body is agleam with sweat, but he is not even breathing heavily. Two long scars flank his eyebrows—souvenirs of elbow punches—and he has a quick, crooked-toothed smile.

"I'm 25," he says. "My parents were rice farmers in Lopburi, but my father had been a boxer in his youth, and taught me what he knew. When I was 11, I won my first fight at a temple fair in Lopburi. I collected 100 baht. When I was 16, I entered a boxing camp in Singburi [hence the nickname] and fought over thirty fights during the next three years—usually at a stadium in Rangsit. By the end, I was earning 5,000 baht per bout.

"When I was accepted by this camp, I started out at 140,000 baht in Rajadamnern Stadium. I've been fighting ten bouts a year since then. I've won fights in London and Seoul too. Each month, I send 30,000 baht home to my mother, who employs ten girls now in a sewing factory. In another two or three years, I plan to retire to Lopburi myself. I go home every couple of months to rest up for a few days after a fight."

And the paycheck for his upcoming bout with Wanwisit?

"Two hundred and fifty thousand baht," he replies, flashing his crooked grin.

○ ○ ○

Wanwisit's camp is more bucolic. The Jockey Gym is a large, open compound down a meandering *soi* lined with wooden houses and fruit trees near the Rama VIII Bridge.

Twenty young men in boxer trunks are playing *takraw*. Some lay around a parlor floor watching soccer on TV; others work out on a Nautilus weight machine. Under a tin canopy stands the boxing ring, and over it are hung twenty framed color photos of former champions: the camp alumni.

Two trainers, Ponsak Sichang and Somchai Suwatdiwichai, jog into the compound and explain that Wanwisit is still off on his afternoon's run. Ex-boxers themselves, scarred and tattooed, both men still keep fit for sparring but allow themselves the luxury of cigarettes.

"This camp—the Jockey Gym—is thirty years old," Ponsak explains. "We train thirty fighters here, plus ten kids in the junior division, as young as 12. Wanwisit was just a kid when he first came here." He reaches down to his knee. "He was that small."

Dressed in a silvery sweat-suit, Wanwisit arrives—his short spiky hair drenched with sweat. He *wai*s and then shakes hands awkwardly.

Two years younger than Nophodej, he is exactly the same height and build. He has an identical scar over his left eyebrow, and a much longer one—11 stitches-worth—high on his left forehead.

Wanwisit explains that he is from a boxing family. Like many of Thailand's folk arts—*manora* dancing, shadow puppetry, traditional music—boxing is an art that is passed down from generation to generation.

"My father was a boxer," he says in a soft, high-pitched voice. "He runs his own boxing camp in Khon Kaen—the Norasingh Camp. At ten I won my first fight and got paid twenty baht. Nine years ago, my father sent me down to this camp. There's another ten fighters from Khon Kaen training here, and some of them are my relatives. Everyone here is from the Northeast. I'd say that 80% of all *Muay Thai* boxers in Bangkok are Northeasterners. I've fought sixty bouts in Bangkok, averaging 220,000 baht now. Last year I won eight fights, losing only once to a boxer named Chaidat."

Wanwisit does not mention it, but he was also voted the Best Boxer of the Year by Rajadamnern's International *Muay Thai* Association. Of his rival Nophodej, he comments, "We're both the same kind of fighter—knee-kicking to the inside. I've got the better punch, I think."

In the compound, the fighters are warming up now. With the younger boxers, there is an air of schoolyard horsing around. Two kids are duking it out in big red practice gloves. Other boxers stand in a circle, joking, laughing, yelping in encouragement at well-placed punches.

By the time Wanwisit and his trainer, Ponsak, climb up into the ring, there is a small crowd watching from the compound's gate: kids on bicycles, squatting old men and giggling schoolgirls. *"O-way, o-way, o-way,"* Wanwisit grunts as he pummels the bejesus out of Ponsak. By the third round, the older man is winded and collapses, laughing, on the canvas. Wanwisit moves to the floor-length mirrors by the gate, shadow-boxing and tossing off jokes to the crowd. He is a national hero.

○ ○ ○

On fight night, the front of Rajadamnern Stadium is a sea of parked motorcycles. Along a row of *Isaan* restaurants are lined the Benzes and Beemers of promoters and high-rollers.

Inside, under the concrete bleachers, the boxers' dressing room is dim, narrow, hot, and reeking of the familiar scent of liniment. Trainers tape the fists of their boxers, stretch them out on massage tables to be slavered in liniment and Vaseline, and fit them into groin protectors.

The atmosphere is informal, with fans wandering through, women and children too. A 'wardrobe lady" is handing out boxing shorts.

Wanwisit straddles a chair as his fists are taped, bantering with his trainers and his manager, Somak Kigaw. Various dignitaries stroll up to offer encouragement. Wanwisit *wai*s them all. Around his neck he wears a priceless Buddhist amulet suspended on a thick necklace of woven *saisin* strings.

In the foyer outside, dressed in jeans and T-shirt, Nophodej stands amid a crowd that is cheering on the final round of a preliminary match down in the center ring. His fight, the Main Event, is the seventh on the bill. He swaps greetings with other boxers, occasionally exchanging playful punches. He seems relaxed, calm to the point of serenity.

The stadium is packed to the rafters.

Krongyut Sukwannakhon, Rajadamnern's assistant manager, is pleased at the huge response to this matchup of Wanwisit and Nophodej.

"Fights like this draw a big crowd," he says in his office. "People come not just to see who can beat who, but to watch how the best boxers can change tactics from round to round. It's important to match up the right fighters. Both Wanwisit and Nophodej are very popular. I especially like Wanwisit's style. He was voted the best fighter last year because he's always going forward and he gives his all. There's a spiritual element of courage—he never gives up. He's an elegant fighter, good with his fists, knees, elbows and feet.

"Some people are good kickers but can't box. Some are good at inside fighting but are useless on the outside. Wanwisit's good at both. Nophodej is the same kind of fighter.

But to heighten interest in this match, Wanwisit took a three-pound handicap. I expect a tremendous fight."

Back in the dressing room, Wanwisit sits on a massage table slavered in ointment, relaxing after a vigorous massage. Ten feet away, seated with his back to him, Nophodej is having his fists taped. Each studiously ignores the other, as they will after the fight, too. *Muay Thai* boxers do not taunt each other during the build-up to the fight. Nor do they do so in the ring. Circumscribed by ritual, *Muay Thai* shuns the boasting, the hype and the theatrics of international boxing.

Wanwiset soon retreats to an alcove outside the room, while Nophodej's trainers leave for the ring with another boxer from the Chu Wattana camp, Muangfahlek Kaivichien, who is favored to win the sixth bout of the night. It's a classic matchup: the handsome, smiling Muangfahlek, a counter-puncher, versus a relentless attacker—the scowling, prune-faced Singhnoi Prasatporn. After a slow first round, Muangfahlek takes the next two easily, then wilts under a ferocious counterattack in the fourth. In the stands, punters wildly wave fingers and hands to signify ever-changing odds: 4–1, 3–2, and back to 4–1 as Muangfahlek dominates the final round. The three judges give him a unanimous decision.

Wanwisit and Nophodej's names are announced and they enter the ring to no fanfare and absolutely no applause. The fans are too busy settling bets. The house band strikes up the music for the *wai kru* dance—literally, the "homage to the teacher." The seven-holed *pi chawa*, or Java flute, makes a martial-like skirl similar to a Scottish bagpipe, and is backed by the high and low toned, male and female, double-headed drums called the *glawng khaek*. A steady rhythm is kept up by the saucer-sized *ching* cymbals.

Wearing *mongkols*—headbands inscribed with sacred scripts—Wanwisit and Nophodej kneel in the middle of the ring, bow to the direction of their birthplaces, and—to the rhythm of the band—commence their dances. Nophodej finishes up first, and then stands rather awkwardly in his corner as Wanwisit continues for another minute. As the music stops, both *wai* their trainers—Wanwisit, his father; Nophodej, his manager—and receive softly-chanted blessings. Then it is time for mayhem.

Muay Thai bouts consist of five three-minute rounds separated by two-minute breaks. The fighters need that much time to recuperate their strength; the punters to negotiate their bets. First rounds are almost always a draw—as the band plays slowly, the crowd is quiet, and the boxers feel each other out.

Bobbing and weaving, seemingly to the rhythm of the band, Wanwisit and Nophodej exchange light punches. Nophodej shoots a lightning kick to Wanwisit's ribs, blocks a return kick, and dances out of danger. He steps in again to deliver two solid kicks to Wanwisit's hips. Wanwisit then swings a high kick, but Nophodej grabs his foot and dumps him heavily on the canvas. After another exchange of kicks, the bell rings.

Round two, and the pace quickens. Nophodej delivers two sharp kicks to Wanwisit's ribs. Wanwisit retaliates with a solid kick—*thwack!*—to his hip. He follows up with a jab that connects to Nophodej's jaw. Nophodej counters with a kick to his stomach, sparking the first applause from the crowd. The two exchange a half dozen more kicks until Nophodej shoves Wanwisit back to the ropes. Wanwisit misses a high kick, then connects again with the jab. Nophodej shoves him back on the ropes and the two swap knee-kicks to the ribs. As the bell rings, the 10,000 fans in the stadium are generally taking 2–1 odds for Wanwisit. The three judges will give him this round too.

Nophodej opens round three with a deft kick to Wanwisit's stomach. Wanwisit retaliates and the two launch themselves into a blazingly-fast flurry of kicks—Nophodej getting in the last one before backing off. They swap jabs and then

Nophodej leaps to the attack, throwing a devastating barrage of foot and knee-kicks until Wanwisit manages to throw him back on the ropes. Nophodej bounces off and flies into the attack again, shoving Wanwisit into a corner and landing a kick to his jaw. It's only a glancing blow but the crowd erupts into a cheer. Wanwisit scores with a left hook but is kicked back into the ropes again. Pandemonium in the stands. When the bell rings, the odds have shifted to 5–4 or 3–2. The judges score this round for Nophodej.

Round four. Nophodej shoots a solid kick to Wanwisit's solar plexus, throws him to the ropes, and dives in with two knee-kicks to his ribs. The crowd roars. Wanwisit lands a strong right to Nophodej's nose, and he backs off. There's a sudden lull as the two trade cautious punches. Then Nophodej sneaks in a quick kick to Wanwisit's hip, and they clinch against the ropes. Wanwisit leaps up to jab a knee into Nophodej's ribs. Nophodej immediately knee-jabs him on the other side. Wanwisit hits back, then Nophodej, Wanwisit, Nophodej, Wanwisit. The music reaches a frantic pitch and the crowd cheers in unison to each kick. The two boxers whirl in a circle—elbowing, and grappling for position—then fling themselves into another flurry of kicks. The crowd roars louder.

As the bell rings, the punters are switching their bets to Nophodej. The judges score this round for the underdog again. In Nophodej's corner there is an air of jubilation. Wanwisit is slumped on his stool being vigorously rubbed down by Ponsak. At ringside, trainers and promoters are angrily shouting up advice. The stands are in uproar as a waving sea of hands places bets.

The bell rings for round five. Nophodej advances to Wanwisit's corner. He attempts a sweeping kick, and Wanwisit plunges in with a straight right jab to the point of his chin. Nophodej's legs crumble and he crashes on his back to the canvas. The crowd screams. The referee starts the count as Nophodej woozily rises to one elbow and flops back down again. The ref shakes his head and sweeps his arms. Knockout. Nophodej's handlers rush into the ring, help him on to his feet, and lead him—wobbly-legged—back to his corner.

In the dressing room, two women are sweeping up discarded bandages and cigarette butts. Four handlers strip a smiling Wanwisit of his gloves, tape, and sopping-wet boxing shorts. Ten feet away, a dazed Nophodej is slumped on a massage table. A dozen friends are crowded around to commiserate. His manager's wife, the movie actress Laiwadee, sweeps in to comfort him. She tells Nophodej that he fought a good fight and was ahead on points going into the final round. "Go home to Lopburi and take a rest," she says. "Go home."

Nophodej nods, tears welling in his eyes.

A Night in the Life
The Bargirls

Soi Cowboy is the poor man's Patpong. Drinkers at its 35 bars tend to be working-stiff residents rather than well-heeled tourists. Soi Cowboy is also the poor woman's Patpong. The go-go dancers and hostesses are almost all economic refugees from the Northeast. Most do not command the premiums that the Northern Thai beauties on Patpong do.

At 6 p.m., the Suzie Wong bar is stirring to life. Go-go dancers arrive in streetclothes, change in the bathroom, emerge in red silk warm-up robes, and kneel on banquettes before the wall mirrors, putting on makeup. Others smoke cigarettes, chew gum, spoon up bowls of *kway-tiaow*.

"*Pee Nok, kin kao?*" one girl calls to a thirty-ish woman at the bar to join her with a bowl of noodles.

"Thanks, I ate already," replies *Pee* Nok. Dressed in a chic, twill suit, Nok sips coffee and checks off entries in a ledger book.

"Excuse me, are you the manager?" I ask her.

"No, I'm the mamasan," she replies coldly.

Over the next few minutes, Nok proves polite but not particularly friendly. The entries she is marking in the ledger book are the arrival times of the dancers and bargirls. Lateness entails a fine, as does taking off more than two days a month. The system is universal. What seems like cacophonous chaos on Cowboy, is really a Thai hierarchy— of owner, manager, mamasan, hostess and go-go dancer— arranged along a strictly-defined *pee-nong* (senior-junior) structure. Everyone knows their place: who to look down upon or up to. The key is money. Many working girls are single mothers, abandoned by their husbands. They are

caught between the rock of obligations to their parents and the hard place of educating their own children.

Mui is an oddity at Suzie Wong: a Southerner from Narathiwat. Southern Thai women seldom work as bargirls. Their claim is that they have too much pride and honor, and that recruiters in the South would be shot. Northeasterners joke that Southerners cannot hack it as bargirls because they are too *peu dam*, *jai dam* (black-skinned and black-hearted). Aside from regional prejudices, a simpler explanation is economic: in the prosperous South, women have no need to prostitute themselves.

Mui came to Bangkok at 16 as a student, but preferred to chase after a career as a singer. Then—and this story is universal too—she met a man. She moved with him to Pattaya, worked as a chambermaid in a hotel, and gave birth to a daughter. They spilt up and she returned to Bangkok in search of work. Along with a girlfriend, she checked out Patpong, felt it was too dangerous, and settled instead at the more friendly Cowboy.

"My daughter is 13 now," Mui confides over a sixty-baht glass of Coke. "She lives with my mother and goes to a good high school. I see her once a week. As a hotel maid, I earned 2,800 baht a month. My base salary here is 1,800 baht plus around eighty baht in tips each night, and 25 baht for each drink customers buy me. I have two nights off a month but I work anyway. It's a struggle to keep up with expenses. I share an apartment with two other girls, splitting the 3,500 baht rent.

"My English isn't good, but I like the customers here. The English are especially polite, but the Germans and the Japanese pay the best. They drink a lot and tip big. I had a German boyfriend who bought me this watch. It cost 20,000 baht. Another time, he took me on a big shopping spree at Robinson Department Store. On the other hand, a Finnish guy took me all around Bangkok for a week, and when he left for his oil rig job in Indonesia, he left me with 500 baht. *Farang* men make all that money—how can they be so cheap?"

The music starts at 7 p.m., and five dancers shuck their robes and climb onto the stage. We are joined by Noi from Khon Kaen.

"I'm 28 and I've been in Bangkok for ten years," she says. "I worked with my husband as a market seller at first, but then we separated and he has custody of my daughter. He doesn't know I'm working here, nor does my father. If he did, he'd drag me back to Khon Kaen. As a dancer I make 3,000 baht a month. If I go off with a customer, the bar fine is 400 baht, with the mamasan keeping 100. All in all, I average about 10,000 baht a month."

"Nobody works harder than Noi," Mui interjects. "She's got a day job as a conductor on a mini-bus."

"That's another 6,000 baht," Noi confirms. "I get up at five in the morning, finish up at two, sleep for four hours, and then come here. I'm saving up to buy a condo. I live alone. I like a quiet life."

"Do other girls have day jobs too?" I ask.

"I guess so, but I wouldn't really know. I don't talk to many people."

I ask Mui and Noi if they see any possibility of bargirls organizing themselves into a union to demand, say, more than two days off a month?

They both shake their heads. "No way," says Noi. "There's too much competition. Too many girls."

"I might ask for 1,000 baht to 'off' with a customer," Mui says. "But other girls will ask for only 500. One guy turned me down to go off with a cheaper girl. 'I don't care what your face looks like,' he said. 'I just want one thing.'"

At 8 p.m., there are only three customers in the bar. One old guy is on a banquette, sandwiched between a bikini-clad teenager and the mamasan. Up on stage, two dancers in matching red bikinis are bumping hips. At the end of a song, one climbs down to the floor. The other grabs her arms and tries to haul her back up. "Dance! Dance!" she cries playfully.

"That girl once got 6,000 baht for one night," Mui comments. "The guy felt sorry for her."

"I had a Canadian boyfriend for three months, but he went back to his wife," Noi says. "He sent me 5,000 baht. He phoned me from Canada, crying, 'I miss you so much.' I said, 'I miss your money.' It's a game."

"One of the girls here wanted to marry another Canadian," Mui adds. "He married a *farang* girl instead, and years later he walked in with his wife. When she saw them, she cried."

Two beefy Germans take stools at the bar. They are quickly surrounded by girls who rub cold towels over their faces, massage their shoulders, and collect Cokes. A pretty teenager in a black dress is talking animatedly with Noi. But there is something strange about her voice. When she leaves, I put the question to Noi.

"Yes, she's a *katoey* [transvestite]. Some guys like it. There's three or four who drift through here. Some have had the operation, some not."

The German owner comes in to collect money from the cashier. I introduce myself and ask if we can talk.

"I don't even have time to read the newspaper," he says, but agrees to meet me the next night.

Outside, the street is abustle with food vendors, strolling foreigners, and bargirls in warm-up jackets calling, "Welcome inside, please sir!" A mustachioed Tom Selleck lookalike swaggers past. "WELCOME INSIDE PLEASE SIR!" screeches a Suzie Wong girl. "Oooh, he's *so handsome*!" she cries, and collapses in a fit of giggles.

A rock band is playing on stage in the middle of the *soi*, courtesy of an anti-AIDS NGO. A raucous audience of bargirls explodes into applause at the announcement of a Miss

Condom Contest. Each of four bargirl contenders demonstrates how to slip a condom over a vibrator.

"This is Soi Cowboy," states one contestant. "We all know what a 'raincoat' is."

"Nobody knows more about AIDS than the women on Soi Cowboy," confirms Chursak Sangpitak, manager of the Crazy Cat bar. He is seated at an outside counter, watching the show. "All the girls get weekly VD tests and, if they're found to be infected, an AIDS test as well."

During the day, Chursak is an English teacher at a prestigious high school. He has been managing the Crazy Cat for ten years, making between 8,000–12,000 baht per month on commission.

"It's not a bad job," he says. "I've learned a lot more English, and I have a chance to help people. Most of the girls are from the Northeast. They're poor, uneducated, and responsible for their families. I try to give them good advice— not to gamble or take drugs, to save their money, and to provide for their families and their future. In the ten years I've been here, half the girls at the Crazy Cat have married foreigners. They have children and are successful. They send letters and photos, and sometimes come back to visit. Others become hairdressers or dressmakers. Nobody really likes working on Soi Cowboy but there's a lot of money here."

At a neighboring counter, a Danish businessman complaining of jet lag is chatting with a stunning, long-haired *katoey*. They leave together. Boy, is he in for a surprise.

"The Crazy Cat used to be the most popular bar on Soi Cowboy," Chursak continues. "That was when all the bars here were just one shophouse wide. Then came the big bars— Darling, Tilac, Butterfly—which were three rooms wide with two or three bars inside. Customers prefer to be in a place with a lot of girls. Some of them are closed or have changed format already. We're facing a lot of competition from the Nana Entertainment Plaza, which has nude dancing. Our regular customers stay loyal to us, though." Chursak points to a sign over the bar-room door which says, *The Customer is the Boss.* "If somebody gets too drunk, we take him home. I take care to make the customers safe. Honesty pays. My idea is that if you eat too much, you vomit. If you eat moderately, you can eat every day."

A huge cheer goes up as the winner of the Miss Condom Contest is announced. The biggest cheer comes from the bar down the street where Miss Condom works.

"I've lived in 14 countries and this is the only one where I can't make money," complains Wolf, a German bar owner. "My Thai wife gambled away two and a half million baht and my lawyer ripped me off. I bought this bar for 900,000 baht. Other bars go for as high as two million per room. A German consortium owns the bigger bars like Tilac and Suzie Wong. The small bars tend to be Thai owned.

"Cowboy was more fun three years ago. We're hurting from the Nana Plaza. That's a different police district. They're stricter here, and it's a low crime zone. I might let my girls dance topless but full nudity is degrading. I always swore that I would never live off drugs or women. And I'm not, really. The girls aren't forced to do this. They're free to go out with guys or not. I didn't create the business, and the pay is good.

"A mother brought her teenage daughter here who'd just finished her contract at a massage parlor. She wanted to sell her daughter for 20,000 baht. I told her to fuck off. There was a crackdown last year on girls working here who were under 18. But the campaign backfired. They're all working as freelancers now—with no VD checks—at all-night bars like the Thermae, which is owned by the police."

I wander outside and find three policemen seated outside the Long Gun, which is another police-owned bar—and the only one on Cowboy permitted nude dancing. The uniformed cop is Tourist Police.

"My job is safety for tourists," he tells me. "I've been on the beat here for a year. There's no trouble; it's quiet, not like Patpong with doormen boxing tourists."

The two regular cops, in mufti, are from Krabi. They drop into the Southern dialect to give a brief history of Soi Cowboy.

A Muslim from Pattani named Sergeant Han—with his pearl-handled Colt .45—had been the law here for many years, visiting all the bars, drinking coffee with the managers, keeping an eye on things. "We're continuing that tradition," says one policeman. "Soi Cowboy is a safe place."

It's midnight back at Suzie Wong now. Two glassy-eyed Japanese men are bobbing their heads to the disco beat. A bikini-clad dancer sits in a customer's lap, engaged in major tongue kissing. Watching the go-go dancers are four stolid Thais with mobile phones. A sleeveless Australian is swigging from a beer bottle. An Italian couple come in and they are greeted enthusiastically by a hostess who gives them each a big kiss.

A timid customer pokes his head in the door.

"Welcome inside please!" cries a hostess.

"Just looking," he says, backing away.

"Thank you for looking. "

"Thank you for letting me look."

I try to ask the mamasan about her job, but she gives me the cold shoulder again. "Talk to the manager," she says. "Why talk to me?"

"Because you're important," I reply. "You probably know more than he does."

"Maybe. But I'm still not giving you an interview."

As closing time approaches, the music switches from disco to *Isaan* folk songs. The dancers sing along. The cashier bangs a tambourine. The mamasan climbs up on the stage and joins the dancers. Mui tells me that Nok had originally been a go-go dancer herself. As Nok climbs down, I engage her in a spastic *ramwong*. She laughs and dances with me for five minutes, and at last says, "Okay! I'll talk to you tomorrow!"

Next day, my interview with the German owner is not a success. He was under the impression that I was selling magazine subscriptions.

"I don't want any publicity," he says firmly. "I had it once and I don't need it. We stop this interview. No other way."

He did venture the comment that the economy of scale of his big bars is a liability when times are bad. But he will not take his bars topless, despite the competition from Nana. "Once the novelty of nude dancing wears off, I expect the regulars to drift back to Cowboy," he comments. "At least I hope so."

And my interview with the mamasan is also a disaster. She stonewalls me, smilingly.

"But you promised to talk to me!" I plead.

"I did. But I won't."

And that, perhaps, is the essence of Soi Cowboy: unfulfilled promise and a hint of mystery.

The Cheapest Thrill in Bangkok

The Express Boat Commodore

On a Tuesday morning rush hour in Bangkok, the Sathorn Pier is jammed with commuters—uniformed students, civil servants in white shirts and ties, office girls in high heels and skirts—who clamber on and off floating pontoons, embark and disembark from a steady stream of express boats. This is the heart of Bangkok. Over the pier, arches the Sathorn Bridge, roaring with traffic. Someday the elevated skytrain will connect to this vital nexus, but for now, commuters here depend upon that most ancient of thoroughfares: the Chao Praya River.

Among the waiting crowd is Supapan Pichaironarongsong-kram. When a white wooden express boat pulls up to the pier, the deckhand and ticket collector *wai* and smile, and then extend helping hands to her as she boards the boat. This is because Supapan is the owner of the Chao Praya Express Boat Company—in charge of a fleet of 92 passenger boats and their crews. Today, she is taking photographer Jonathan Taylor and I on a trip up the river.

"Boats have been our family business since my grand-mother came from Chiang Mai to live in the palace of King Chulalongkorn," Supapan says, as the boat swings upriver, past the flowered balconies of the Shangri-La Hotel.

"That was eighty years ago. She started the first cross-river ferry, and would often have to settle fights between boatmen. Her four sons all became civil servants. In the thirties, my mother, Supatra, wanted to go to Thammasat University, but the family didn't have the money. So Supatra expanded the ferry service. The family legend is that she sold a cigarette box studded with rubies to buy the first engine for a ferry. She eventually graduated with a law degree from Thammasat and married when she was 34."

Supatra's two daughters—Pattaravadee and Supapan—grew up swimming together in the Chao Praya. The younger Pattaravadee became famous as a model, movie actress and show business producer, while elder daughter Supapan had a roundabout education—in Thailand, Switzerland, England and the United States—before returning to work for Firestone in Bangkok in 1966. She took over the express boat service in 1971, at the age of 26.

Express Boat 201—in which we are cruising—is one of a newer design: larger and faster, seating 120 passengers rather than the usual 70. We glide between the Oriental and Peninsula hotels, then past the Sheraton; the River City complex; the Ban Chao Praya condominium; the riverside mansions of the French and Portuguese ambassadors; churches, *wats* and Chinese temples; and assorted ramshackle wooden buildings.

"On September 22nd, 1971, we started with 23 boats and 77 employees," Supapan recalls. "Five years after we started, I remember how happy I was that we had made 8,000 baht in one day from 3,000 passengers. We handle up to 50,000 passengers a day now, and operate 41 piers, 71 express boats, 21 cross-river ferries, and have over 400 employees. I used to know everyone in the company, but I don't know the newer ones now."

Soon we pass through the Chinatown of Yaowarat, stopping at the big pier at Rachini Market, where Chinese and Indian faces predominate. The boxing ring of a training camp stands out over the river; mosques intermingle with Buddhist temples; a riverside restaurant is sheltered by a line of palms. Under the twin Prapokklao and Memorial bridges, we come to a bend in the river. Up ahead looms the glittering *chedi* of Wat Arun. On the same shore, the Royal Thai Navy is headquartered in a restored Sino-Portuguese building painted mustard yellow, with twin verandahs. From a flagpole atop a whitewashed fort bristling with cannon, flies the navy's white elephant flag.

"Often a husband and wife team work together on the same boat," Supapan continues. "The husband is the captain, the wife the ticket collector, and a son might be the deckhand. After an apprenticeship, he advances to be trained as a captain too. It's a whole lifestyle. And it works out well because if the wife is the ticket collector, she gets a percentage of the take. This way the captains don't drive their boats too fast. The families live in four company compounds on the river, paying us a sliding scale of rent—400 to 100 baht—diminishing with length of service."

On the right bank of the Chao Praya, we steam past the magnificent spires of Wat Pra Keo and the Grand Palace. On the left bank, we come to Ban Khunying, the traditional riverside home of Supatra Pichaironarongsongkran, who died five years ago, aged 83. Here her daughter Pattaravadee puts on theater entertainment every Sunday. Supapan also plans to open a restaurant here, and a museum to her mother—with all proceeds going to the Supatra Foundation, which provides education for needy children. "This will be a memorial for my mother," Supapan says. "She loved boats, and she loved the river more than life itself."

We pull up to Mahatat Pier, where Express Boat 201 will stand down until the afternoon rush hour. We chat with the captain, Sompong Sukra, 42, who has been with the company for twenty years. Like many captains, he is from Nonthaburi. He started out as a deckhand, and demonstrates the whistle signals with which he used to guide the captain to dock: one blast to stop, two to reverse, four to go forward. Captains start off at 5,500 baht during a four-month probation period, earning up to 7,000 baht before retirement at age sixty.

Three ticket collectors—Supapin, Kanda and Pipalam—say they are happy with their lives aboard boats. Supapin and Pipalam are both married to captains. They earn a base salary of nearly 5,000 baht, plus monthly incentive payments of 800–1,000 baht.

Supapan leads us to the headquarters building of the Chao Praya Express Boat Company. In the lobby is a model of a steel express boat, Number 180.

"This is our only steel boat, designed by a Thai navy architect, but it proved too heavy and expensive to operate," she explains. "The rest of the fleet is made of wood. Originally they were all made from teak, but when this became too expensive, from a local wood called *ton kien tong,* which is very strong—as it needs to be, banging up against piers all day. I'd like to build five new boats, whether from our old design or from new ones I'll be looking at—I don't know.

"There's a boat show in Singapore soon. I'd like our service to be faster and more comfortable. The work itself will be done at our boatyard in Ayuthaya, at Ban Pan, a village which is famous for its artisans. They shape the hulls in such a way that they lift high off the water, cutting down friction and increasing speed.

"Looking to the future, I don't see my 12-year-old daughter taking over the company. The business has gone beyond us as a family. The company must either go public, or be handed over to the government. I'd like to focus more on tourism development of the river. This I why I launched Supatra Tours, to organize weekend boat trips."

From Mahathat Pier, Jonathan and I continue upriver toward the terminus at Nonthaburi. Hopping an ordinary 70-seater boat, we speed between Thammasat University and Siriraj Hospital. During the student demonstrations in 1973 and 1976, Supapan told us, her company had rushed extra boats to ferry wounded students across the river to the hospital.

We cruise under the Pin Klao Bridge and dock briefly at Phra Athit Pier, crowded with Western backpackers from

Khao San Road. Further upstream, we pass the white fort and riverside park at the end of Phra Athit Road; moored rice barges; apartments; and pastel-colored, wooden homes up on stilts. Kids dive off front porches. Market women paddle skiffs past new condominium towers. We pass under the Krong Thon Bridge, flanked by big riverfront restaurants.

The land levels out, becomes green and open, and a giant can of Singha Beer announces the Boonrawd brewery. Three giant copper brewing vats—dating back fifty years—overlook the river. Past the Rama VII Bridge, we head into the last stretch of river for the Express Boats—past Wat Tuk, Wat Kien and Wat Khema—and come to the clocktower and gingerbread Victorian provincial hall of Nonthaburi.

At the floating Rim Fung restaurant, old men sit before fishing rods and glasses of *Mekhong* whiskey. Jonathan and I order a slap-up seafood lunch which, together with beer, comes to less than ten dollars. Our whole time on the water was little over an hour, but it encompassed the very soul of Bangkok.

And the cost of our trip?

Eight baht—less than 25 cents—for the cheapest thrill in the city.

Hog Hell
The Klong Toey Butchers

You smell the slaughterhouse in Klong Toey long before you reach it—blood, offal, and very bad drainage—and you hear it too: the hellish screams of unhappy porkers.

Under neon lights in fifty wooden pens, young muscular men, barechested and barefooted, hack away with machetes and cleavers. This grim work is a family affair that goes back two and three generations.

"Almost all of the butchers here are Catholic," says Fr. Joe Maier, an American priest who came to Klong Toey in 1966. "Sixty years ago, the diet of most Thais was still rice and fish. It was the Chinese who created the big demand for pork. They started up the first slaughterhouse near Hualamphong Station and recruited Vietnamese Catholics for the work. Then, about forty years ago, they moved the operation to Klong Toey, which, at that time, was well out of the city. There wasn't even a road here. In charge of the slaughterhouse community was a French priest—Fr. Maurice Joly—and he said Mass for the Vietnamese families under a bridge. Our church now has 100 families, many still in the old pig-killing trade."

The trade is a lucrative one, tightly controlled by the Livestock Association of Thailand. Fifty Sino-Thai merchants own the pens, and the ten to 15 workers in each pen are paid piece rate. They make around 200 baht for a night's work.

"It's the old *tokay* system, which places value on worker longevity and loyalty," reports Fr. Maier. "The stall owners are generally good for a 500–1,000 baht loan when a family falls into trouble."

The pigs are delivered in the morning and the killing starts around 8 p.m., and can go on until the very early hours, with the fresh carcasses being trucked out to about 135 city markets for further dismemberment.

It's a pig rush hour on a Friday midnight. In one pen, fifty fresh corpses hang from overhead hooks. At the opposite end, fifty doomed live porkers stand cheek by jowl, looking away from the frenzied work in the middle of the pen which they don't seem to want to know about. Suchat, 17, smokes a cigarette and estimates he will make 250 baht tonight. He wears a slingshot around his head to keep away stray dogs. His 12-man team—sweaty, dripping wet, clad only in soggy shorts—work fast. They form a precision-tuned machine that turns, in bare minutes, 100kg hogs into pork.

A worker snags a pig by the mouth with a stevedore's hook. His partner grabs the tail and a hind leg and the two flip the screaming hog onto an iron-pipe trestle where a third man yanks back the left foreleg to expose the throat. A fourth butcher darts in to jab a long knife in and upward for a two-foot gash. Blood geysers everywhere. The pig stops screaming only when a fifth worker whacks it over the head with an iron club. He's dumped into a tub of boiling water, plucked out and scraped hairless by two men with cleavers who toss him to the ground where one guy cuts off his head and another two hook the hind tendons and hoist him upside-down on chains for disemboweling. The guts are slid across the floor where a kid wraps them in twine and drops them into a vat of hot water. The pig's body joins the rest of his mates on the meat rack.

The concrete floor is slippery with blood, guts, and water. The men are constantly hosing down both the pigs and themselves.

On a fence outside the slaughterhouse, a Protestant Evangelical group has posted a sign in Thai: "*The Blood of Jesus Washes Your Sins.*"

A Tale of Two Restaurants

The Restaurateur—Sara-Jane Angsuvarnsiri

"The first time I met my husband, Chai, it was hate at first sight," recalls Sara-Jane Angsuvarnsiri.

"I was at Simmons College in Massachusetts and the girl across the hallway from me was Thai. We got to be good friends. On Thai holidays, I'd go with her to parties in Boston. Chai was in his last year at Northeastern and was president of the Thai Students Association. Every time we met, we argued over everything. If I said something was white, he said black. Constant debates.

"Then he asked me out to dinner and I thought, 'Great. I'm really going to stick him for an expensive restaurant.' We had dinner at a nice Italian place and he was perfectly charming. Dr. Jekyll and Mr. Hyde. Stop that. Stop running."

The last two comments are directed at Sara-Jane's four-year-old son. Relaxing at the poolside of the US Information Service (USIS) compound on Sathorn Road after a tennis game with her teenage daughter, Sara-Jane points a finger at the boy who has just come skidding to a halt. "What happens when you run?" she asks.

"You fall down."

"Right! Anyway, Chai and I would go out dancing or to the movies. Three months after he went back to Bangkok, I joined him and we got married. His parents weren't too happy. They're Thai-Chinese and I think their main concern was that we were young and in love, but eventually I'd become unhappy here and go home to the States.

"It turns out we get along great. I learned Thai as my kids grew up. At the family compound, I'm the dutiful daughter-in-law. I make cakes, cook, host parties, take family visitors

59

shopping and sightseeing. I've changed here. I have more respect for elders. Friends say I'm more Thai than American. I think I've become less self-centered and more understanding of others. My parents-in-law taught me a lot."

"Can I have ice cream?" her son asks.

"Sure," she sighs. "But after my two oldest daughters — 15 and 13 now—went off to school. I was going nuts with nothing to do. Chai was working in the family business: chemicals, paint, printing and import-export. We thought of going to the US and opening a Thai restaurant, but decided to open one in Bangkok instead to get the experience.

"My education in Thai was intense. None of the staff spoke English. At first, I stayed out of the kitchen to avoid conflict, but then I began making suggestions like how to marinate and cook chicken so that the skin is crunchy and the flesh is moist, or how to cook beef so that you keep the juice. *Isaan* people cook meat to death. Look at you. You've got ice cream all over you."

Sara-Jane wads up a napkin and wipes a long streak of chocolate ice cream off her son's forearm. "Go and wash. *Not* in the pool. In the bathroom. We decided to open an *Isaan* restaurant on Soi Lang Suan because there just weren't any decent ones around. Sara-Jane's Restaurant—seating 150 in two air-conditioned rooms—was a success from Day One. Lunchtimes, it's always packed. A Channel 3 television crew came in one day and wanted to film me. I was petrified. I hate video cameras, so I said no. They said, 'What?' so I told them, 'Go ask my husband.' Chai, damn him, said to go right ahead. They filmed me grilling chicken in the kitchen, and I swear that chicken weighed fifty pounds.

"TV announcer Maw Song was an old customer, and he was mad because I'd refused before to be filmed for his show, *Tom Pai Du*. So I did his show, too. This time, the chicken didn't weigh so much. Maw Song showed a long segment about the restaurant on a Sunday afternoon and that night the place was a mob scene. We ran out of chicken, the staff was confused, bills got mixed up. It was hell.

"Running a restaurant is a seven-day-a-week job, but I love it. In August 1987 we opened another Sara-Jane's—an Italian restaurant on Convent Road. My husband and I really like Italian food but, in those days, about the only good Italian restaurants were in hotels, and they were very, very expensive.

"My idea was to open an Italian place that wouldn't cost an arm and a leg. Our prices are still very reasonable. We got started because a Thai friend had quit his job as an Italian chef. He was used to cutting corners, but I put a stop to that. No watering down the sauce.

"Eventually we moved from the townhouse on Convent Road to a big, forty-year-old house on Sukhumvit Soi 26. It's got real crystal chandeliers, a garden, plenty of parking space, three dining rooms, and two private rooms upstairs.

"After shutting down the old restaurant, we had about three weeks to get the new one ready: widening the gate, tearing down walls, setting up the kitchen, new dishes, silver-ware, glasses, tables, chairs and seat cushions. A very hectic time—a challenge—but I enjoyed it. The new restaurant doesn't look Italian; it's me—light and airy—with many Thai paintings.

"We have a lot of friends in the art community. I particularly like Tawee Kesa-Ngam and Sangnard. Artists here normally get a pittance from gallery owners, who then sell their paintings for a fortune. They're true artists—impoverished, living from day to day. I hang their paintings for sale in the restaurant. It's good for them and it's good for us. The restaurant is always changing.

"I usually work in the *Isaan* restaurant for lunch, then go to the Italian one for dinner. In the *Isaan* restaurant, I'm in the kitchen in shorts and a T-shirt, cooking up a storm. Then I head home, meet the kids as they get out of school, shower the grease out of my hair, and put on a dress and make-up for the dinner trade. Once, I was in the *Isaan* kitchen and the staff from the Italian place called to say that 'Big Su' had just come in."

Two of her daughters approach with a dispute. Sara-Jane settles it, and, with a veteran mother's ability to handle the kids without missing the continuity of an adult conversation, takes up the story. "I wasn't sure just who 'Big Su' was, but I went over anyway. I didn't bother to change clothes. I was wearing shorts and T-shirt and my hair was a mess. 'Big Su' was General Suchinda [Kraprayoon]. This was right after his military coup and he was, indeed, big. I apologized for my appearance. He said never mind. He was very nice.

"Another time, 'Big *Suea*'—'Big Tiger,' General Pichit [Kulavanijaya]—came to the *Isaan* restaurant. I happened to be wearing a shirt embroidered with a big tiger's head. It turned out that his wife really liked the shirt and I promised to get one for her. I did, too.

"We get a lot of movie stars. Michael J. Fox and Brian De Palma ate at the Italian restaurant, just up from filming in Phuket. I really love this business. I've met a lot of people that I wouldn't have met otherwise, and I've made a lot of friends. Get him out of the deep water!"

Her son, hanging on the back of another child, is twenty feet out from the shallow end of the pool. They turn and head back, faces wreathed with grins of smug triumph.

"Don't you ever take him out into the deep water. You know he can't swim. My kids are 15, 13, 7 and 4. Three girls and a boy. The girls go to St. Joseph's School. I wouldn't send them to the International School, much less to an American high school. I like the conservative Thai schools. Maybe they'll go to the US for university or post-graduate studies.

"In 16 years, I've been back to the States five times. My oldest daughter came with me three times, the second twice, the two youngest once. My in-laws stayed with us in Worcester and my parents came to Bangkok three times. They get along fine.

"One thing I've noticed about old friends in the US is how stressed-out they are. I work hard but they tell me I look like I'm still in high school. I tell them that it must be the weather, but really it's just the easy way of life. They ask if I'll ever come to live in the US again. I tell them that Thailand has spoiled me: maid, cook, nanny for my son. In the States, I'd have to come home from work and clean the house too. Thailand's taught me a lot, but it's also spoiled me.

"My restaurant staff has been great, too. Many of them have been with me from Day One. Sometimes people leave, but then they come back. They miss the family atmosphere. I mean that literally, since everyone seems to be related to each other. I've lost track of who is whose cousin. The *Isaan* restaurant is one big Northeastern family; the Italian from the Central Plains.

"People ask me why I run an Italian restaurant when I'm not Italian. 'Why not?' I reply. I run a Thai restaurant and I'm not Thai. Put that down. Put that down right *now. . . .*"

Battle of the Palates

The Journalist (Reporter's Notebook 1)

"The blending of a great wine is often considered an 'Art,' and for centuries winemakers have strained their seasoned palates and noses in their quest to create wines of great charm, balance and complexity."

Thus read the invitation to attend Bangkok's first Jacob's Creek Shiraz Cabernet Blending Seminar. On the evening of the event, a select 100 guests lined up behind ranked tables and wine samples at the ballroom of the Regent Hotel.

Up on a giant screen, by the miracle of a satellite bounce, chief winemaker, Philip Lief, appeared live from Australia. He paused throughout his introductory speech on the interactive video to allow Thai translation of his "*pasah* (language) *Australia*".

Australian wine is big business. Worldwide exports have grown 20% over each of the last five years, and Australia holds a 25% share of the Thai market. As for quality, Australia humiliated France at the 1996 International Wine Challenge in London, winning 31 gold medals compared to 28 for the French who had three times as many entries.

Jacob's Creek is the leading exporter; its one million cases representing a fifth of Australia's total. Our task was to blend two cabernets and two shirazes to match the Jacob's Creek Shiraz Cabernet, voted best Australian red wine of 1996.

On the giant screen, Philip Lief pointed out four wine growing regions on a map of Australia. Coonawarra near Adelaide, and Riverland near Sydney, are the sources for the two cabernet sauvignons we will sample.

South Australia's Barossa Valley and Langhorne Creek produce the two shirazes.

Philip characterized the shirazes as, "soft, full, rich, velvety, and plummy." The cabernet sauvignon, he said, was "an austere wine," with the Coonawarra strain flavored by its oak barrels. We dutifully sampled the four wines. The Regent's in-house video zoomed in on the audience—serious suits, sniffing and sipping.

"Your task now is to mix these four wines to match your sample glass of Jacob's Creek Shiraz Cabernet," announced Philip. "None of the four wines will comprise less than 10%, none over 50%, and, since this is a *shiraz* cabernet, there will be more shiraz than cabernet in the mixture. The winner—whoever produces the best match-up—will be awarded his or her weight in wine."

We bent to our laboratory beakers and funnels, tipped our four glasses, and spilled a lot on the white tablecloths. The serious suits beavered away with their beakers, each showing the fanatical intensity of a Dr. Frankenstein. Purple wine stains spread wider.

"Doctors now say that two glasses of wine a day is good for you," Philip intoned from the screen. "Four is better."

"I want to know how you get rid of wine stains on tablecloths," said the lady journalist next to me, surrounded by purple puddles.

"Eighty or ninety vintages can go into a blend like this," Philip continued.

"God! Think of the laundry bills!"

On my other side, to my great good fortune, were seated two sisters, Kulvadee and Korakoj Kulanet, who do indeed know their wines.

"Wine tasting is a passion in our family," said Kulvadee, senior manager at the real estate firm of Jones Lang Wooten. "Our father was half-French, and owned a shipping company. There were new wine shipments all the time. He taught my sister and I how to drink, so men couldn't get us drunk and in trouble. I began sampling wine at 14. I've lived in Italy, Germany, Australia, and California, near the Napa valley. Any place I go, wine is my friend."

The sisters gave me their blends to sample. Both glasses smelled and tasted identical to the Jacob's Creek Shiraz Cabernet. Mine tasted like vinegar.

We handed in our tote sheets. Kulvadee chose a mix of 20% and 15% cabernets; 35% and 30% shirazes. Her sister made it 25% and 15%; 35% and 25%. I've got it all wrong: 20%, 10%, 30% and 40%.

Up on the screen, Philip announced the correct formula: 21% and 17% cabernets; 35% and 27% shirazes. Moments later, two winners were summoned to the stage. One was Korakoj. She was weighed, and awarded four cases and two bottles of Jacob's Creek Shiraz Cabernet.

"I told you to go on a diet," Kulvadee said when her sister returned to her seat. "Now everyone knows how much you weigh."

"Fine," Korakoj replied sweetly. "That's just more wine for me."

Streetwise

The Sidewalk Food Vendors

Sometimes it seems that half the people in Bangkok are cooking and serving food to the other half. Or that Bangkok is one big alfresco restaurant. Find a crowd—any time, anywhere—and vendors line up their pushcarts bumper to bumper.

Chantana Kajaisi catches people right off the river, as they come off the express boat at the Oriental Hotel pier. Her deluxe four-wheel cart—the Cadillac of the breed, costing 6,000 baht—serves up a half dozen species of fried fish, sausages, fried eggs, liver curry, mixed vegetables, porkball soup and *gaeng som* (mullet in sour sauce).

Chantana, 48, a Bangkok native, has been manning her stall for over ten years. "I used to be a kindergarten teacher," she relates with a smile. "I started helping out a friend here and when working the two jobs became too much for me, I became a vendor full-time. I live in the outskirts of Bangkok, in Ban Mok, and I get up at five each morning for the hour's trip here. My husband and a friend help me shop in a market nearby, and then we cook up the food for the day. We start selling around seven in the morning."

Besides the flow of express boat passengers, Chantana's steady customers include clerks at the East Asiatic Company next door, students from Assumption College down the *soi*, a rotating crew of motorcycle-taxi riders, and a few random tourists.

"Germans mostly, for some reason," she observes. "Maybe I'm in their guidebook. I serve well over 100 people per day and am generally sold out by two or three in the afternoon.

Then we clean up and lock up the stall and head home in time to serve dinner to my son. He's 16 and a student at a technical college. I make a profit of 7,000–8,000 baht a week plus, of course, free food. Sundays I take off. Holidays too, when I want. I like the freedom. But it's still not enough money!" she laughs. "And food prices are rising."

Stroll up Silom Road to Soi 3 and you will find Somnuk Poonchak and his wife at their barbecue stand. Another Bangkok native, Somnuk serves up perennial *Isaan* favorites: barbecued chicken and fish, sticky rice and *somtam* (papaya salad). He does a roaring lunchtime trade, his four sidewalk tables packed each day with office workers.

"This is a part-time job for me," Somnuk says. "I'm actually a civil servant. My wife and two teenage nieces do most of the work. We get up when it's still dark, shop at a market near our home, pile everything into my car, and a half hour later, at six in the morning, we're open for business here. I go to my office around nine and come back late in the afternoon to pick up the family.

"We store the cart overnight in a place nearby." Somnuk waves a hand to a drinks cooler and cigarette display case. "With beer and cigarette sales, and take-away food, we make over 10,000 baht a month."

The King of the Silom street vendors is Ratree Jitcham. His huge cart on Silom Soi 1, opposite the Taniya Plaza, is an iced-down cornucopia of fresh sea bass, mullet, mussels, cockles, squid, shrimp, oyster, cuttlefish, king prawn, blue crab, horseshoe crab, conch shells and rock lobster. His wife runs a neighboring noodle soup stall where Ratree, this Saturday evening, is carefully laying out strips of liver and beef over a bed of ice.

The air is thick with smoke from boiling cauldrons of soup and a rank of four charcoal braziers. Ice buckets are crammed with beer, soft drinks, and even a couple of wine bottles. Two dozen sidewalk tables await customers.

"I came up to Bangkok four years ago from Nakhon Si Thammarat," Ratree recalls. "As a Southerner, I know seafood. I'd been running my own restaurant in Nakhon Si Thammarat, but I had this idea to set up a top-quality street stall in the heart of Silom Road. It's worked out well. My three daughters work with me, and another dozen kids from Nakhon. Every afternoon at five, I arrive in my pickup truck and we get set up for the evening trade. From now until two in the morning, we'll serve 500 people. Our seafood couldn't be fresher. We get daily truck deliveries from Mahachai pier in Samut Sakhon, and special items like oysters and giant prawn from Surat Thani. I make a profit of around 50,000 baht a week."

Is he bothered by Bangkok's traffic and pollution? Does he miss the South?

Ratree shakes his head and grins. "Hey, I'm happy for the money."

As in all businesses in Thailand, success spawns imitators. Down the street, opposite Patpong Road, is another sidewalk extravaganza—opened by Roi-Et native Pahsuk Plongkai. His rolling restaurant sprawls over the plaza of the Southeast Asia Insurance Company. Pahsuk is out of town tonight, and the task of supervising a staff of 15—Pahsuk's relatives and friends, recruited from Roi-Et—has fallen to manager, Suchat Gaiyai. Seated at a rear table with a busy cashier, Suchat keeps an eye on four teenage girls tending a row of braziers. Fish, wrapped in aluminum foil, steams underneath, while racks of squid, crab, conch shells and giant prawn are prepared for the flames. At another table, more girls shell oysters and mussels; slice lemons; and chop onions, garlic and scallions. Waiters in shorts and T-shirts rush up to hand bills to the cashier tapping away on his calculator.

"We average well over 300 people a night," reports Suchat. "Plus another fifty *farangs* from Patpong across the street. We've developed a good reputation. We start selling at six, and cater to a big office trade—especially on Friday nights when people gather to eat and drink and wait out the traffic before going home. Weekends they come back with their families. There's also a rush around midnight from Patpong. We close up at one, pack everything into pickup trucks, and take it to the owner's house on Soi Suan Phlu."

Suchat, a Bangkok native, observes the bustle around him. Teenage cooks and waiters scurry about frantically, laughing and joking. "These kids are from Roi-Et, a very poor province, and they're happy to be here," he comments. "They're not rich Bangkok-Chinese who can afford the huge rents for restaurants, but they make the best food. You go to the Gaysorn Restaurant on Sathorn Road and shrimps are 650 baht per kilo. Here it's 250 baht. And it's the same shrimp! No such thing as a rich man's shrimp! I'd estimate we make 5,000–6,000 baht profit every night. Except when it rains, of course. Then everything goes back into the freezer at Soi Suan Phlu.

Besides the weather, does he have any special problems? Say, with the police?

Suchat and the cashier throw back their heads and roar with laughter. "We *are* the police!" Suchat shouts. "Altogether, you got seven cops working here!"

But to descend from Silom's gastronomic Big Time, let's consider a far more typical street vendor—away from the hordes on Silom—a traditional neighborhood peddler of that all-time Thai favorite, *khao moo daeng* (red pork and rice). Sixty-two-year-old Ekkasit Malaithongthae has been a street vendor all his life—first in Bangna and for the past 11 years in Banglamphu, Bangkok's oldest neighborhood.

On a weekday morning, Ekkasit is in perpetual motion, slapping together the ingredients of *khao moo daeng*—plain rice topped with roasted red pork, crackling, duck egg, sweet sausage, cucumber slices, scallion, a thick sweet sauce—and dispatching dishes to a half dozen tables.

"We open at six in the morning for the breakfast trade, and close down between two and three," Ekkasit explains. "My wife and I have a girl who helps out. She does the shopping for us in Banglamphu market each morning. We have plenty of regular customers from nearby government offices and banks and factories. I guess I make *khao moo daeng* for over 200 people a day. Plus another thirty or forty take-out packages."

Ekkasit's eldest son works at the Siam Commercial Bank down the street. His younger son, Kulachart, a student at Bangkok Commercial College, is serving tables on his summer break.

"My parents take the weekends off," Kulachart comments. "We could work seven days a week, because on weekends Banglamphu is packed with shoppers, but my parents are getting old and prefer to take it easy. As it is, we probably make a daily profit of over 1,000 baht. And our house is just down the alley here, so parking the pushcart is no problem."

The pushcart itself is a hefty, chrome-and-tile work of art. "This cart is over thirty years old," Ekkasit comments proudly. "I bought it then for 1,000 baht. It's worth many times that now."

Rivaling *khao moo daeng* in Thai fast food popularity is *khao kah moo* (pig's leg and rice). Around the corner from Ekkasit's cart is the pig-leg mama, Supawadee Purdpee. Heaped atop her bubbling cauldron of sweet pork sauce is an oleaginous mass of pig meat—a mix of fatty pork and just plain fat that must be a cardiologist's nightmare. And, like everything that is bad for you, it tastes great.

"I've been working at this stand for seven years now," says Supawadee as she wraps up a take-out packet of *khao kah moo* for a mother and her little girl waiting on a bicycle. "I bought a second-hand pushcart and suddenly I was in business. I open around seven every night and close up at one o'clock. I only live three blocks away, so pushing the cart is no problem."

Collecting thirty baht, Supawadee hands over the *khao kah moo* packet to the mother on the bicycle. As she peddles off, her daughter's sandal falls to the street. Supawadee snatches it up and shoves it back on the girl's foot. "Mom worked hard for this shoe!" she scolds, laughing. "Lose it and she'll beat you!"

Further down Chakrapong Road is the night's culinary mainstay: the four-wheeled pushcart of Siriporn Naymin. Siriporn displays no less than 14 big serving trays containing fried fish, duck eggs and fatback, cabbage and pork, minced beef, *gaeng som, som tam,* chicken curry, spicy mussels, green beans and peas, and mullet in basil leaf—plus five pots of coconut glass-noodle desserts. Depending on Siriporn are the neighborhood's *mae tung plastic*—the "plastic bag mothers"—working women who, after a hard day at the office and bucking the traffic home, have no time to cook for their families. Into the breach steps Siriporn.

"I've been doing this for three years," she says as she deftly scoops different sauces into plastic bags. "My husband and I are retired civil servants, and this is a way to stretch our pension by 400–500 baht a day. Maybe fifty people come to eat here each night, but well over 100 come to pick up takeaway dinners. I shop in the market in Thewat, cook at home, then load everything on my pushcart for sale at around six. By midnight, I'm generally cleaned out."

By the time Siriporn is going home, Montri "Moo" Chokechai is just opening up shop. If Ekkasit is on the day shift and Sirporn on the night, Moo is definitely on the graveyard shift. As a seller of *khao tom* (rice porridge), Moo caters to a late-night drinking crowd. On Wisut Kasat Road—in an area of bars, nightclubs and comedy cabaret cafes—weary revelers spoon up Moo's *khao tom*, mixed with boiled eggs, sausages and pickled vegetables: the traditional end to a long night out with the boys. Moo often stays open till 5 a.m. Occasionally, people fall asleep at his tables or wander off without paying.

"Are there ever any fistfights?" I ask.

"No, no, never!" laughs Moo. "I don't know if they ever fight in the bars or nightclubs, but by the time they come here for *khao tom*, they're trying to sober up—getting ready to face the wife at home!"

By the time Moo has gone to bed, breakfast vendors like Chantana and Somnuk are already buying a new day's food in the market. And so goes Bangkok—an unending, movable feast.

Vital Signs

The Deaf Vendors

The lunchtime scene in the school courtyard seems typical: kids gather around picnic tables, play volleyball, kick *takraw* balls, and shoot basketballs. But instead of the usual youthful din, there is absolute silence. This is the Deaf School on Soi Suan Phlu—these kids talk with their hands.

"We have 228 students, from kindergarten through to high school age," explains principal, Jitprapa Srion. "Our school opened in 1961 and we're funded by the Special Education Department. We're part of a network now of 12 Schools for the Deaf nationwide. The students here learn the national sign language—adapted from the American system developed at Gallaudet University in Washington—with additional vocabulary for the Thai alphabet and Thai concepts. For more sign language words, we can look to the *Thai Sign Language Dictionary* compiled by the National Association of the Deaf in Thailand [NADT]."

One out of every 500 Thai is prevocationally deaf—that is, deaf before adulthood. A first-time visitor to Bangkok might be forgiven for thinking the proportion much higher. Deaf street vendors of clothing and handicrafts are highly visible in the tourist areas of Sukhumvit, Silom, Patpong and Banglamphu where—with hand-held calculators and appealing smiles—they have no problem driving hard bargains. A visitor might also conclude that so many deaf vendors are part of a single conglomerate, organized perhaps by an NGO. But this is not the case.

"There are two NGO associations for the deaf—the NADT and Friends of the Deaf—but they're not involved in this

enterprise," states *Ajaan* (senior teacher or professor) Jitprapa. "And the various vending groups simply don't cooperate. They can't communicate with each other. I mean, they *can* through sign language, but their ideas differ. They don't take advantage of opportunities to unite."

Instead, the proliferation of the clothing and handicraft vendors is a simple example of copycat capitalism. Informal cooperatives in different locations buy clothing in bulk, and then sell at individually-owned stalls. According to Anucha Rattanasint, president of the NADT, the pioneer entrepreneur in this field was Vichai Limsikan, a Laotian from Nakhon Pathom, who opened the first clothing stall at Sukhumvit Soi 11 over twenty years ago. Vichai also took a leading role in founding the NADT. Begun as an informal alumni association for deaf school graduates, the NADT was formally registered as an NGO in 1984.

Anucha himself is a clothing vendor on Silom. A volunteer sign language teacher for four years at NADT headquarters on Silom's Soi Pan, he was elected president by the ten-member NADT executive committee. Through an interpreter, Anucha explains that the NADT has 700 members in Bangkok and 800 in the provinces—with branch offices in Chiang Mai, Khon Kaen, Songkhla and Phuket. In July 1995, the NADT sent delegates to Vienna for a conference of the World Federation of the Deaf.

Of the major groups of clothing vendors, Anucha estimates that fifty are at work on Sukhumvit, over forty on Patpong, thirty on Silom, twenty in Banglamphu, and over twenty in Pattaya. There is also a large contingent of vendors in Phuket. In Chiang Mai, a group of deaf entrepreneurs runs a drinking-water distributorship.

Anucha functions as informal leader of the Patpong/Silom vendor contingent, fostering cooperation and settling disputes. Of his customers, he estimates that 70% are Western tourists, 20% Japanese and other Asian visitors, and 10%

Thai. "They [the Thais] know our prices are too high," he signs with a smile.

His sign language for foreign nationalities demonstrates a sly wit. Australians are two bouncing kangaroo forepaws; Germans, a finger over the head for a spiked helmet; English, a pound note sign; French, steepled fingers for the Eiffel Tower; Japanese, a rising sun on a samurai headband; Indians, a *tilak* sign and a waggling head; Americans, ten fingers locked in unity; and Israelis, a hand cupped over one eye for a Moshe Dayan eyepatch. He characterizes Israelis and Indians as being difficult to bargain with.

Turning to the work of the NADT, Anucha enumerates regular courses in Thai sign language and Thai literacy education. There are vocational skills programs, a handicrafts factory, nationwide deaf clubs, an illustrated NADT newsletter, and a video news program distributed through the Schools for the Deaf network. The NADT coordinates with the government and specialized NGOs for the promotion of programs for the deaf, and holds a representative seat on both the National Council for the Disabled, and the National Council for Social Welfare. The NADT has played a major role in drafting legislative proposals for a "Comprehensive Rehabilitation Act for the Disabled in Thailand."

"The bill addresses discrimination against the handicapped," says Anucha. "Our agenda is to develop vocational skills, and to open up job opportunities for the deaf. The law will fill a social need—as there are positions we could fill in industry, but factory owners doubt our ability. We want equal rights."

Besides social gatherings organized by the NADT, Anucha adds that the Patpong/Silom deaf community meets informally each day at MacDonalds (mouth chomping a fist-hamburger) or Kentucky Fried Chicken (fingers stroking chin whiskers). And every Sunday afternoon, a city-wide gathering of the deaf happens on the sixth floor food center of the Mahboonkrong Shopping Center.

On a recent Sunday afternoon, nearly 100 deaf people—students, courting couples, old people and children—were grouped around tables, earnestly conversing in sign language. At one table, Suthep Kasemcharoensuvi, president of the Friends of the Deaf, drank coffee with *Ajaan* Jitprapa and four Australian teachers from Melbourne's National Institute for Deaf Studies and Sign Language Research. "This is a regular social event," *Ajaan* Jitprapa notes, gesturing around the food center. "But it's also a learning experience: people teaching other people how to communicate better."

Visiting her table were a wide cross section of Bangkok's deaf community: Nippon sells electrical goods at Mahboonkrong; Suthep works on his father's rice farm in Talat Noi; Somsak, a Bell computer expert, is headed for an advanced course in Japan; while Sumali makes 300–500 baht a day selling clothing on Silom.

Anucha Rattanasint and a group of Silom vendors have bigger ambitions. They are buying a bar on Patpong.

Hayley's Confessions

The Backpacking Bar Hostess

Hayley Pugh—23, tall, lithe, blond and English—strides into the Banglamphu guesthouse she had left seven months ago to work as a bar hostess in Osaka.

"I was amazed at my first Japanese club," she recalls. "It was so *posh*. Deep-pile carpet and red velvet, statues and mirrors all over. A sign said 'To the Toilet' and you went through a long narrow coridor to a door and beyond was a scene from Dante's *Inferno*: smoke and noise, buxom blondes dancing topless, and Japanese men stuffing wads of yen down their G-strings. The Yakuza sat at stage-side tables with *mountains* of money in front of them. The dancers made 250 pounds a night. I got 15 pounds an hour for sitting at tables, pouring the men's drinks and lighting their cigarettes. At eleven I'd be hustled out before the real business got started. It was the biggest *gaijin* brothel in Osaka.

"I quit after two weeks to take a hostess job at a respectable bar. I made 450 pounds a week, which may sound like a lot, but out of that I was paying 80 pounds for rent and 100 for food. Also, I had to fly back to England for my grandmother's funeral, which took a chunk out of my savings. I'm not complaining. I've got quite a bit saved. It's not as much as a few years ago, though. In those days, Western bar hostesses made a fortune."

Hayley Pugh was on her way south for a long vacation on Koh Phangan, Surat Thani's premier hippie island. "I need to chill out," she smiles.

Four weeks later, tanned and rested, Hayley agreed to an interview at the Ton Poh Restaurant, overlooking the nocturnal boat traffic on the Chao Praya River.

"I'd been teaching English in Bangkok for six months when I met an Australian girl named Tanya on Koh Samet," she recalls. "She described working as a bar hostess in Osaka—pouring men's drinks, lighting their cigarettes—and it seemed an awfully easy way to make a lot of money. I made a living wage as an English teacher, but that was it. I needed a grub stake to travel on around the world.

"The first place I worked, The Amber Club, was in the South side of Osaka—*Yakuza* territory—sleazy but glamorous. There were three hostesses, five topless dancers and four hookers who made top dollar and dressed spectacularly. They were all tall, busty Californian blondes with silicone implants and tanning-room tans and fabulous bodies from working out. They were saving money to get on with their lives. Loretta worked in a cop outfit for her strip show. She did three shows, three minutes long, and made US$75 in tips each time. Pia wore a cowboy hat and spangled shorts. Very *short* shorts. She'd grab the ties of the Japanese men and whip them around their necks. They went crazy for her. She showed me photos of a huge house she was building in California with a gym and heated pool. The hookers could make 5,000 pounds a night. I admired them really. They could have sex with ugly, repulsive men and still stay whole and sane. They struck me as strong women, with high self-esteem.

"Two weeks later, I moved to North Osaka, to the upper-middle-class entertainment district and a club called *Eikokukhan*, or 'English House Pub.' Wood-panelled walls, plush velvet banquettes, glitzy chandeliers, a jazz band with black American singers, Brenda and Cathy—big mamas who belted out the old favorites like 'Kansas City'. Sometimes a Japanese customer would take the microphone and sing horribly and we'd all applaud madly.

"Everything was strictly ritual. When you pour a customer's drink, you have to look into his eyes and say in

Japanese, 'Permission for me to drink?' Then you clink glasses, making sure to keep your glass politely lower than his, and say, '*Kampai*,' which means 'Cheers.' If you say, 'Chin chin' that means, 'Little dick'—big joke.

"There were 23 Western girls in my club. Fifteen were Australians, the rest Swedish, Brazilian, a New Zealander, Israeli, English, French and two Filipinas. We were the largest *gaijin* club in Osaka. There were two other big clubs and perhaps thirty more that had a few Western hostesses. Altogether, say a couple of hundred hostesses in the city.

"There was a lot of pressure from management to pump up the business, and a lot of competition among the girls to attract regular customers—all sorts of cliques. I didn't get involved in that. A cute, submissive type is the Japanese preference. A loud voice and speaking your mind is *not* appreciated.

"The dress code was very strict: chiffon and velvet dresses, high heels, nylons, lipstick with lip liner, perfectly-shaped nails, not a hair out of place. There was a strict hierarchy too—from the owner to the manager to the mamasan and down to us. The mamasan is very important; she's seen a lot, she's hardened and respectable, and she pulls the club together. She handles difficult, even violent customers, and makes everyone feel welcome. She's got a degree is arse-kissing.

"When customers arrive, the mamasan's at the door with the manager and the waiters, all bowing and exchanging ritual greetings and welcomes. The customers were seated with drinks—always *Mizo*, whiskey and water—and dishes of nuts. Then they either summon their favorite hostesses, or the manager would pick a couple of us to join them. We went up and bowed and said, '*Hinshai mase*,' which is 'Welcome,' and '*Genke deske*,'—something like 'Happy healthy'—and tell them our names. If they're still talking business, you stay quiet. The job takes diplomacy, tact, social skills. When they're ready to talk to you, it's the same questions: 'Where do you come from?' 'For what purpose did you come to Japan?' (To make money, of course, but you make something up). 'How long have you been here?' Of course, they hardly speak English, so this comes out, 'How time?. . . 'Many long?'. . . 'How month?' 'Five months,' you answer sweetly. Then there are a string of dumb, simple jokes. Whoever the table roars with laughter at, that's the boss or prospective client. You learn the politics.

"Customers are charged for the table and for the hostesses' time. I didn't like the rigmarole, the artificiality of the situation. Paying for friendship. Some girls had a genius for pretending. The star was Megan, an Australian who towers over me, and I'm six foot. She had a trick of gazing rapturously into the men's eyes. Another star was Cilla, an Israeli, who they thought was exotic.

"The stars would have one or two customers a night. I averaged five a week. If you averaged less, the management cut your wages. There was constant pressure for you to go out to dinner with clients too. The quota was four a month. For each one you failed to make, you were fined 5,000 yen. For the privilege of taking you out to dinner, customers paid about 8,000 yen—the cost of the table at the club.

"The men are sad. They're drunk and pathetic and lonely. They always say they love you but it's bullshit. We gossip about them. There are six types:

"The bore. He can't speak a word of English but thinks he can and you spend three hours saying, '*Honto*?'—'Really?'—like your life depends on it.

"The pompous old-school Japanese. He knows exactly what kind of service he requires and he'll complain to the manager if you don't measure up—pour his drink the wrong way.

"The young hotshot. He's out to impress you. His English might not be so bad and you can have a bit of fun.

"Weirdos. I always got them. I remember Ito-*san* who was grim and drunk and said the same thing thirty times in a row. 'I want to get you a video machine and what's your address?' I never did give it to him.

"The lonely hearts. They come alone to the club and complain about their wives. You feign interest. They talk, you listen.

"The lecher. He's obnoxious and will grope and paw you and shower you with mental abuse. We all hated that type. Customers will normally hold your hand or give you an occasional peck on the cheek. Anything more was frowned on.

"Customers normally come in groups of two or three. Bills of 200,000 yen—US$1,700—aren't uncommon. One single guy spent 600,000 yen in one night.

"We worked six nights a week, from eight till two or three. Afterward, we'd go out together for a drink or just go home and watch a video. It would take me till around five in the morning to unwind—till I felt like myself again. It was the mental strain that got to you. It's the most bizarre experience I've ever had. I'd get up in the late afternoon, go shopping or to a vegetarian restaurant. I didn't see much of Japan. I went to sessions at a yoga meditation center three times a week. This helped against all the stress I was under. Sundays, our nights off, we'd wear our grungiest jeans and rave all night in an acid house.

"There were basically two types of girl in the hostess business. Travelers like me—up from Koh Phangan and Khao San Road—were just in it for a few months to pick up traveling money. Other girls, mostly Australians, were working there for a couple years. They learned Japanese and taught English during the day and were saving up to buy houses in Australia and to open up businesses with their Japanese language and contacts. Sometimes they'd move in with a customer and make twice what they did as hostesses.

Or, if the customer was married, they'd be set up in an apartment.

"But basically, it all came down to greed. We'd be sitting at the entrance to the club, tapping our feet, and saying after half an hour, 'Well, we've just made another 15 bucks. Thirty Australian dollars an hour was more than most of us would make in a day."

Hayley was born in Birkenhead, near Liverpool. At age eight, she moved to Malta where her father was working on oil rigs. "That gave me a taste of the sunny life," she observes. Two years later, she was back in England, a village in Somerset. She was accepted into the prestigious Maidstone Art College, south of London, but gave it up to travel through Europe and the Middle East. To finance her travels, she worked as a sewing machine operator, tent maker, gardener, waitress, barmaid, stagehand, and a model in Israel.

Back now from a month of strenuous partying on the beaches of Koh Phangan, Hayley feels restored to her old free-wheeling self again. She hopes to meet an old Israeli boyfriend in India next. She'll buy silver there, do some trading in Europe and Japan, and eventually make her way to South America. "For the longest time, I've been going with the flow," she reflects. "Haven't decided yet what to do with my life. Getting tired of it, actually."

Would she go back to hostessing in Japan?

She shakes her head. "Just a few years ago, Western hostesses were like goddesses in Japan. But now that the economic bubble has burst, there's less money for that kind of nightlife. At the same time, many foreigners are going to Japan to work. It's supply and demand—and the pay has gone down."

Screen Play

The TV Producer

Convent schoolgirl, TV hostess, jet-setter, full-time mother, and documentary-showbiz impresario, MR Supinda Chakraband has managed to cram five lives into one. Her birth foretold a life of footloose wandering.

During World War II, a Swedish ship bearing 17 Bangkok-bound Thai students from the US pulled into the harbor of Lourenco Marques, Mozambique. By the time the ship docked, the Thai contingent numbered 18. MR Supinda was born. "And I've been drifting ever since," she laughs.

Her father was Prince Chakraband, who had recently graduated from Cornell University; her mother was Mom Vibra Chakraband, from the University of Michigan. Family legend has it that when Prince Chakraband had his first awestruck vision of Mom Vibra's beauty, he fell off his chair. "But then, except for music, he was always badly synchronized," MR Supinda says wryly.

Both her parents majored in agriculture. Prince Chakraband went on to become rector of Kasetsart University, and a pioneer of Thailand's agro-industry. Mom Vibra was a highly-revered Kasetsart professor. Both were happiest out in the field. Prince Chakraband delighted in taking students into the countryside to view His Majesty the King's rural development projects (*Chai-pattana*).

At the age of ten, MR Supinda was plucked out of Bangkok to accompany her 13-year-old aunt to a convent school in Switzerland, where her uncle happened to be ambassador. The convent was in Fribourg, on the border of French and Swiss-German speaking cantons. To complicate matters, the nuns were Irish and were learning French along with their

students. "I don't know what sort of English accent I have," adds MR Supinda, "but I hope it's French."

Winter holidays were spent at another convent in St. Moritz, where the band of thirty students could ski until curfew, although MR Supinda notes that, "I'm not a particularly good skier, being physically unbalanced—and probably mentally as well." After another year's study in Paris, MR Supinda was summoned home to Bangkok. Her first job was at the front desk of the Erawan Hotel. Then she followed her aunt to work at Air France.

Then she came across the true love of her life: television.

She stumbled into the job by chance. At a Bangkok reception for the then homecoming Miss Universe, Apasara, trilingual MR Supinda was cajoled into handling questions from the foreign press. This led to an offer from TV Channel 5 to host a half-hour interview show called *Travelogue*. Between 1963 and 1968, MR Supinda interviewed celebrities passing through Bangkok: Sean Connery, Neil Armstrong, Dean Martin, James Garner, Johnny Mathis, Pat Boone and Jane Russell.

This was before the era of mass airline travel and, as MR Supinda recalls, "The world was still small then." To educate her audience about the outside world, she would interview foreign ambassadors and narrate, in Thai, travel documentaries about their home countries. All this was done live, in black-and-white.

Live television had its perils. On one occasion a visiting American choir turned up at the studio, the members lined up in their places and—as air time loomed—awaited an introduction by their hostess. But MR Supinda was off at a birthday luncheon for a friend, having completely forgotten the appointment.

Only when she made a casual phone call to the office did she discover her mistake. She jumped into her car, raced for the studio—where the program director was frantically pacing up and down—sprinted onto the set, snatched up the microphone and launched into her introduction with scant seconds to spare. She laughs at the memory. "I loved that job."

MR Supinda also hosted a half-hour musical variety show called *"Kita Lila,"* featuring Thailand's top singers of the day, like Savalee, Suntraporn and Tony Aguilar—whose daughter Christina would become the country's favorite songstress twenty years later.

But MR Supinda gave it all up after her marriage to a Malaysian business tycoon. She moved into a five-story Victorian townhouse in Chelsea, London, and gave birth to a daughter and a son. She also studied Japanese for four years at the University of London. The lifestyle soon paled. "The life of a jet-setting tycoon was not for me. Flying off to a friend's yacht in the Bahamas one day, off to Paris the next. . . ."

Eventually she filed for divorce, let go of her Thai cook and Filipina nanny, and devoted herself to becoming a full-time mother. "This took some adjustment. I was always buying my children new clothes, because I couldn't wash the old ones quickly enough."

Ten years later, in June 1991, with her son at university in Scotland and her daughter a fourth-year medical student— "The kids outgrew me."—MR Supinda decided to return to Thailand and the work she loved: television.

Again, she came to it in a roundabout way. Her daughter, Anantini, would spend her summer vacations working at Rajavithi Hospital, where she was brought face to face with the specter of AIDS. The horror stories she told her mother galvanized MR Supinda into producing a three-hour documentary for Channel 9.

The first part gave the historical background of the disease—from the birth-control pill and the sexual revolution of the 1960s to the Vietnam war and GIs on R&R in Thailand, to the 1980s tourism boom and the mass commercial sex industry. The second episode dealt with protective measures against the disease, and featured interviews with medical experts. The final installment focused on how to live with AIDS victims in the Thai cultural context, replacing fear of contagion with traditional compassion and affection. Remembering how Princess Diana's televised visits to AIDS patients helped to change British attitudes toward the disease, MR Supinda requested the same from Her Royal Highness Princess Somsavalee, who promptly invited a group of AIDS victims to the palace.

With the success of her documentary, MR Supinda's production company, Oscar, then produced a half-hour drama about AIDS for the Thai Red Cross. *"Pien Kae Khwam Khaojai"* ("Only Understanding") was shown on Channel 7, and fifty copies of the 30mm film were distributed country-wide at temple fairs. Written and directed by MR Mannop Udomdej, and based on a true story, the movie follows the fate of a Thai civil servant who contracts the disease from a former lover, now a prostitute.

MR Supinda then launched the weekly TV magazine show on Channel 11, *"Prungnee"* ("Tomorrow").

"The theme of the magazine was 'What do we do about tomorrow?' It's time for all Thai people to think seriously about the future. The idea behind *Prungnee*, and Oscar itself, is to provide the public with information about such issues as the environment in a *sanuk* [fun] way. The magazine comes across not as the audience's teacher, but as its friend."

Instead of macro-economic issues, *"Prungnee"* concentrated on the many small ways the general public can contribute to restoring the environment. One five-minute segment of 26 episodes, presented by actor Chonprakan Chandruang, *"Kan Chon Gahp Chonprakan"* ["Bumper with Chonprakan"] taught auto safety lessons through comedy. The show was co-hosted by a policewoman who provided serious commentary.

"She was a very attractive policewoman," MR Supinda adds with a smile. "A car key can mean many things: a way to go to work or to play, a status symbol, and also a cause of death. We concentrated on the little things. If you're in traffic, for example, don't use your rearview mirror to apply lipstick."

"*Anusawari Hayha*" ["Fun Monument"]—another slot in the show—was a play on the words *Anusawari Chai*, or Victory Monument. MR Supinda's camera crew mingled with the huge crowds that gather at the Victory Monument traffic circle. People were asked their opinions on the issues of the week, and there was also some wholesome goofing around. "We brought in a very sexy model in a see-through outfit and got people's opinion on the new fashion."

The TV magazine closed with a serious five-minute commentary on the week's news.

Leaving her office on Phaholyothin Road—tastefully furnished with items from her London townhouse—MR Supinda drives her Citroen towards the Victory Monument. Asked if she knows what victory the monument commemorates, she laughs delightedly.

"I don't!" she cries. "And that'll be the first question we'll ask on the next show."

Life in the Fast Lane

The Motorcycle-taxi Riders

Necessity, the mother of invention, breeds *ad hoc* solutions to Bangkok's problems. Just as a legion of mobile phone users has circumvented the phone line shortage, so has a mushrooming fleet of motorcycle-taxis come to the rescue of Bangkok's traffic-stalled commuters. These solutions, however, pose their own dangers. The claim that mobile phones cause brain cancer remains highly dubious, but death on two wheels is all too real.

Of the million plus motorcycles in Bangkok, 100,000 serve as taxis. Countless others are used for small freight transport and messenger services. Convenient? Yes! But the problem with motorcycles is that people fall off them—regularly. Car passengers are surrounded by steel, but for motorcycle riders, as the Thai saying goes, '*Neua hum lek*'—'Their skin covers the steel.'

The bad odds for motorcycle riders are borne out by statistics compiled by Traffic Police Inspector Phrom Dathumma. Over the past six years, the number of people involved in Bangkok traffic accidents has increased from 19,745 to 46,743. Half of these, Inspector Phrom estimates, are motorcyclists. "These are the ones who are most seriously injured," he says. "Twenty percent prove fatal."

Still, until helipads are installed on the roof of every office building and condominium, what alternative is there for hard-pressed commuters but the motorcycle? The gridlock scene is all too familiar: four lanes of cars stranded like beached whales with schools of two-wheeled minnows darting between them, reforming into a solid phalanx before the next

traffic light, engines revving, ready at a flash of green to race down a rare patch of open road.

At peak hours, riding a bike can mean getting to your destination or not. Faced with an urgent appointment and terminal gridlock, businessmen in suits, civil servants in uniforms, socialites in cocktail dresses, all have no choice but to clamber onto the pillion of a motorcycle-taxi and be whisked, weaving wildly, through the rows of immobile steel.

And into whose hands do they entrust themselves?

Generally speaking, a speed-crazed teenager.

Sporting numbered vests, long hair and earrings, the taxi bikers are stationed at makeshift benches all over the city. They while away their time by smoking cigarettes, reading comics, playing checkers. Fares escalate according to distance, traffic conditions, and passenger gullibility. It is a seller's market.

Motorcycle taxis have traditionally plied the *sois* off the main roads, taking commuters the last mile or so home. The drivers on Sukhumvit Soi 31, for example, have set up shop beside a corner building. The eight-man group, organized by a rotation system, takes turns ferrying passengers down the *soi* for ten or twenty baht. According to Daeng, the group's leader, the Soi 31 boys average about twenty passengers on weekdays, less on weekends. Counting long-distance passengers, they earn a daily 300 baht, minus thirty baht for fuel.

The move out onto the main roads was prompted by the traffic implosion of recent years. A busy nine-man group under the Taksin Bridge on Sathon Road does a brisk rush-hour business for commuters coming off the Express Boat Pier. Ton, 25, has been in the taxi business for two years. Five or six passengers a day—going as far afield as Sukhumvit Road—gives him a daily income of 300–400 baht, with 200 on weekends. This allows him to support a wife and son, and keep up the 2,200 baht monthly payments on his 120cc Suzuki.

The concrete benches alongside the Central Chidlom Department Store serve as headquarters for a highly-organized group of 18 bikers. New members pay 1,000 baht for the privilege of wearing the group vest. Each member also pays the group leader fifty baht a day to handle the police. Motorcycle-taxis exist in a legal limbo. While *soi* taxis are tolerated, street taxis fall under heavier police scrutiny.

"There's nothing to stop the police from driving us away from here," points out Pitoon Sirichat. Hence the police "fees".

At 38, Pitoon is older than most of the Central Chidlom riders, half of whom are still single and living with their parents. Like most taxi riders, he is from the Northeast—Udon Thani. Five or six long-distance passengers a day give him an income of 300–400 baht.

Two of his colleagues, Nit from Chumphon and Ott from Khon Kaen, join in a conversation about the benefits and perils of their profession. Both have been taxi riders for three years, and have paid off the loans for their 120cc Yamahas. Nit made a down payment of 15,000 baht and paid additional monthly installments of 3,000 baht over 15 months to secure his 60,000 baht bike. Ott put down only 8,000 baht and took two years to pay off 2,200 baht installments for the same bike. Both are satisfied with their monthly incomes. "I've had other jobs but this pays the best," says Ott. "I like the independence. I feel happy in this job."

As for the dangers of the road, all three riders have fallen off their bikes once, suffering only minor injuries. "The biggest danger on the road is rich ladies in big cars who don't know how to drive," jokes Pitoon. "They don't give us any leeway, and shove us aside."

Pisit Wiriyasakun, a Muslim NGO worker for twenty years, offers some insight into the life of motorcycle-taxi riders. His involvement with the trade began in 1988. In charge of a rehabilitation program for Muslim narcotic addicts, he found employment for 15 ex-junkies as a motorcycle-taxi group in Yannawa. His interest has since spread citywide.

"I'd estimate there are 50,000 uniformed motorcycle-taxi riders in Bangkok," he says. "They regularly pay 'fees' to the police. Another 50,000 don't wear vests and work on a part-time, freelance basis. Half are from Bangkok, 20% from the Northeast, and the rest from other provinces. There are thousands of small groups and no overriding organization."

Pisit disputes the popular notion that motorcycle taxi riders are young. "Seventy percent are between 25–40," he says.

But whatever their age, most passengers would agree that they drive fast. *Very* fast. One common way of dealing with this adrenaline-addled threat is for a commuter to select a regular motorcyclist who drives at a sedate speed.

Trapped in his car on a Sukhumvit *soi* for over an hour, and late for an important dinner party at the Oriental Hotel, a young Danish businessman negotiated a fare of 150 baht from a motorcyclist and then told him, "If you drive slowly and get me there safely, I'll pay you double."

A Canadian journalist, who has been riding his own motorcycles for a quarter of a century, flatly refuses to take a motorcycle-taxi. "In Toronto, back in the sixties, I was riding in a cab when my girlfriend lit up a joint. The driver threw us out, saying, 'If I have to get busted, it'll be for my habit, not yours.' The same rationale goes for motorcycles. If I have to get killed, I want to be in control of the handlebars."

Some of Bangkok's yuppies are doing just that—taking to the streets on their own motorcycles. These are not dinky little two-stroke bikes, but 400–750cc four-stroke power-houses: the Honda Steed, Yamaha Virago, Suzuki Intruder, Kawasaki Terminator. Sleek, low-slung classic models, they sport raked front forks, upswept pipes, teardrop tanks, and an infinite variety of handlebars—from T-bar to ape-hanger—all with leather throttle-grips trailing thongs that whip in the slipstream. Serious bikes, they come in basic black-and-chrome—no raspberry-lime-cherry candy colors. They are a major lifestyle statement.

"There are well over thirty shops selling these motorcycles in Bangkok," notes Nittaya Chankiktcharoen, manager of the Motorhead store on Lan Luang Road. She has seen a shift in big bike popularity in recent years from motorcycle aficionados to ordinary young businessmen.

The big yuppie bikes, not made in Thailand, are shipped by containers from Japan. One- or two-year-old models are classified as second-hand, thus qualifying for a 20% tax break from the usual 90%. Nittaya offers an eight-year-old 750cc, drive-shaft Yamaha Virago for 90,000 baht; and a brand-new 1,500cc Kawasaki Motorhead for 240,000 baht.

Patumwan's Ban That Thong Road, and the warren of *sois* and sub-*sois* leading off it, are a motorcycle Mecca, chock full of showrooms, spare parts and repair shops. On nearby Chulalongkorn Soi 5, the PRT shop sells a Suzuki 750cc Intruder for 170,000 baht; a Honda 400cc Steed for 125,000 baht; and a new Yamaha Virago for 120,000 baht. A monster of a 1,500cc Kawasaki Vulcan goes for 200,000 baht.

In the end, there *is* a simple solution to Bangkok's traffic. Just fork out your 100,000 baht or so and saddle up your Steed, Virago or Terminator. Be the envy of your friends as you roar past them in traffic. But just remember to keep up your medical premiums.

Brit Bikes are Back!

The Journalist (Reporter's Notebook 2)

Fear.

That was Boonprasom Sirivongse's reaction when he first mounted a 900cc Triumph Thunderbird. And quite understandably. Reared, like most Thai, on small motorcycles, he found handling a 220kg superbike to be something else.

"For the first couple of days, I practiced figure-of-eights before I got used to the feel of the big bike," Boonprasom recalls. "Now I'm in love with the Thunderbird. In fact, I'm looking for an even bigger bike now."

Boonprasom and his partner, Roy Barrett, have set up Thunderbirds (Thailand) Ltd., with a mandate to import the full range of new Triumph models: the Speed Triple, Daytona, Trophy, Adventurer and Tiger. They range in size from 750cc to 1200cc. The queen of the fleet, in terms of style, is the Thunderbird, an avatar of the classic Triumphs of three decades ago: the 500cc and 650cc twin-engine streetbikes with clean flowing lines, tapered gas tank, upswept pipes, and distinctive red-and-black finish. The Thunderbird inherits their sweeping elegance, but with a throaty, three-cylinder 900cc engine.

Motorcycles are a matter of taste. BMWs might be marvels of German engineering, but I find them ugly. The American Harley Davidsons, of course, have their own mystique. But to my mind, the British Triumphs of the sixties and seventies were the prettiest motorcycles ever made. When the company went belly up in 1980, legions of fans were left bereft.

Triumph is back. In 1990, a new high-tech breed of Triumphs began rolling off the assembly line at Hinckley, Leicestershire. Annual production of around 40,000 bikes are

distributed to over thirty countries. To bring the Brit bike back to Thailand, Boonprasom and Roy unveiled the newest Triumph model at a Superbike Convention at the Siam Square Novotel. The Daytona T595 howls up to 10,700rpm, generating 128 horsepower on the way. Its fuel injected, in-line three-cylinder engine is a hefty 955cc, yet the aluminum trellis frame adds up to a curb-weight of just 198kg.

"The new Daytona is one of the next generation of motorcycles," comments Service Manager Greg Hondow at the Triumph showroom at Lard Prao 107. "It's got just incredible press. The factory is turning out seventy T-595s a day and they're sold out through all of next year."

Greg began racing Ducati dirt bikes when he was 14 in his native Sydney. He's been a Ducati man ever since. "When I first heard about the new Triumphs, I was skeptical," he admits. "But now I'm a believer. The new Triumphs are great bikes. And they're *strong*—long lasting. In one test, a Triumph engine was stripped down after 250,000 miles. The only part that had to be replaced was the cam chain. And if you compare the Thunderbird to the classic bikes of the seventies, the only similarities are the nameplate and the fact that it runs on two wheels. Frame, water-cooled engine, brakes, clutch, forks—everything is different."

The Daytona T595 sells for 520,000 baht; the popular Thunderbird for 385,000 baht. There is no question in my mind which one I would choose. I go for beauty over engineering any day. I fell in love with the Thunderbird at first sight.

I was even more ecstatic when I accompanied Greg and his assistant, Supak Chobdlama, on a test drive to Khao Yai National Park. Greg was breaking-in a new Tiger, the 900cc off-road bike. Supak and I rode Thunderbirds.

Supak led the way through murderous traffic. Although the son of a farmer in Trat, Supak has ridden bikes in Bangkok for ten years and knows all the moves. In the stalled, bumper-to-bumper parking lot that was Lard Prao, the Thunderbird's bulk and 2.25 meter wheel-base proved no advantage in maneuvering, but once we were out into the moving traffic of Viphavadi-Rangsit, we blasted off.

The Thunderbird's precision steering and huge acceleration power had us swapping lanes with ease and barreling along faster than the traffic. When the slightest hole opened in traffic, Supak would zoom through it, followed at his heels by Greg and myself. The beauty of a big Triumph is that once you pass a vehicle, it is *never* going to catch up with you.

"It's always better to go faster than the traffic," Greg said at a lunch break. "That way you don't have to be worrying about what's coming up behind you."

On the old highway that runs along the *klong* to Nakhon Nayok, we could finally crank up to full sixth gear power. At a sedate cruising speed of only 112kph, the tachometer read 4,000rpm—leaving yet another 4,500rpm till the red line. If I let Greg get 100 meters ahead of me, an eighth-of-an-inch squeeze on the throttle would hurl me up beside his rear wheel in seconds. It was the pure exhilaration of speed: nothing in your ears but the sweet whine of torque. And with its low-slung seat and curved handlebars, the Thunderbird is a very rider-friendly bike—a far cry from the chunky boxcars of the nineties.

We reached Nakhon Nayok in an hour and a half—a trip that takes three hours by tour bus. Speeding through town, we took the side-road that leads to the mountain range harboring Salika Waterfall. The road rose abruptly, twisting into serpentine curves. A sign advised reducing speed to 40kph. I was doing ninety. "Don't touch that throttle," the bike said. "C'mon, lay me into the curve."

The Thunderbird cornered superbly. I heeled the bike into another curve, then dipped, soared, curved left, curved right, flew up a steep slope and down a sharp downhill hook. Mountains are made for motorcycles.

Back on the highway to Prachinburi, we easily topped 120–130kph—and there were endless reserves of power where that came from. We reached Prachinburi at 5 p.m., after two hours of total road time. At 9:30 the next morning, we rode north to Khao Yai National Park.

"Keep an eye out for elephant shit," I warned Greg and Supak. "A friend of mine lost his bike to a big pile of the stuff."

The road snaked higher and higher into the mountains. Except for the occasional pothole, the three bikes barely slowed down as they clung to hairpin turns. The air was rich with the earthy smells of moisture and vegetation and. . . elephant doo?

We braked at the summit of Khao Yai, then plunged down the back side of the mountain and emerged—after 80km of torturous roads—into the rolling foothills of Pak Chong. The home stretch, through Saraburi and down the flood plain to Bangkok, was pure highway bliss, ripping along at 130kph through three wide lanes. Rarely did a car overtake us.

Fighting through a last labyrinthine tangle of Bangkok traffic, we pulled up to the Triumph showroom at 3:50 p.m. Our run had stretched to 330km and it was time now to return to humdrum, pedestrian life. Supak dropped me off at the junction of Lard Prao Road and I gave the Thunderbird one last, lingering look. I could not resist putting fingertips to lips and slapping a kiss on the gas tank. "Goodbye, sweetheart," I said.

Little bikes are like light petting. A Thunderbird is an orgasm.

Lost In The Funhouse

The Light Wizards

In weeds and rubble off Rachadapisek Road squats the wreckage of the giant Phoebus rocketship. The fuselage of this once sleek disco is dirty, sun-blistered, rain-stained, a refuge for rats.

With a wigged-out crew of 10,000 teenagers, Phoebus had once soared high in the Bangkok firmament, only to crash and burn in the Great Bust of 1997. But before the spaceship was launched in February 1995, I had shared the cockpit with Captain Barry Arnold and other techno-wizards who were struggling to get the big bastard up off the ground.

○ ○ ○

"There's nothing like this in the world!" Barry Arnold exclaims, sweeping an arm up at the 1,250 lights—strobes, pin-spots, ring lights, synchros, samurai, robot mobiles—on a 25-meter-wide circular rig dangling from the space dome of the Phoebus Amphitheater. On computer commands, the rig breaks up into eight sections around a center ring that tilts, bobbles, jiggles and zooms forty meters down to the dance floor.

"This rig is the equivalent of five Broadway shows," adds Barry, a New Yorker, who should know, having directed the lighting for *Godspell*, *Ain't Misbehaving, Bubbling Brown Sugar,* and *Joseph and His Amazing Technicolor Dream Coat*. "The system is so advanced that the biggest problem is computer programming. The lighting rig itself was installed by Light Sound Design, headquartered in London. President Chris Cronin flew to Bangkok to see it and had just one word to say: 'Awesome.'"

The Phoebus Amphitheater itself is fairly awesome. The concept is a gigantic Starship Enterprise where a crew of 400 waiters in spacesuits attend to nightly crowds of 10,000 teenagers swilling 2,900-baht bottles of Johnny Walker Black. Up to 15,000 pack in for concerts on a stage that rises, rotates and snakes out into the audience. A second-level observation deck curves around the dome, topped by VIP rooms with charming hostesses. Outside, a 200-table beer garden stays open till dawn.

The technician's booth is on the second level, opposite the stage, overlooking the dance floor and a sea of empty tables on this late afternoon in January. Barry Arnold is huddled with John Willemse, Laser Division Manager of A.V. Systems, and John Goss, a laser designer. Their job is to link together a multi-million dollar collection of space age gadgetry: Show/CAD computer program, Korg mini-keyboard, Phantom laser mixer, Pani wall projector, Yamaha sound-mixer console, Akai master computer.

The Show/CAD software is meant to bring all components into SMPTE —Synchronized Motion Picture Time Exchange— a computerized clock that will dictate by mini-second each light-laser-sound effect which will then be stored on a gigabyte magnetic optical disc.

"The idea," explains John Willemse, "is that you can store an eighty-minute show on this disc, slip it in and walk away. The challenge now is to get all these computers to talk to each other. You call the manufacturers in Japan, England, Australia, and ask if their computer is capable of doing what we want. They call back to say yes and ask me to fax them the results. Nobody's done this stuff before. No manual can tell you how."

"It's a technical nightmare," adds Barry. "The same as launching a Space Shuttle. But it's the best toy any kid ever got for Christmas. Now if we can just make it work. . . ."

They have 19 days to get the system ready for the Grand Opening of Phoebus.

Preecha Chomphupol, A.V. Systems lighting engineer, arrives late.

"Preecha is a world-class electrical genius," Barry says. "He single-handedly set up this system, practically, with support from his boss Ponlawat, who pushed for the best there is and got it from the owner, Charn Platinon, who wanted the biggest and best in town. A place like Phoebus is only possible in Bangkok. The Thai lead the world in this kind of entertainment technology."

John Goss is projecting random laser images around the hall: dancing pink pigs, the Mona Lisa, flying bats, a spinning globe, a giant three-dimensional head of Frankenstein.

"I can make lights come out of his eyes," Barry volunteers.

Preecha is ready to do a dry run of the ceiling rig. John Goss is set to program the lasers. The sound system erupts to the opening of the *Theme to Terminator*. The center disc descends toward the dance floor, wobbling and tilting like a moon-landing vehicle.

"It's too slow!" Barry objects. "How long's the music?"

"Five minutes."

"It takes five minutes to get the fucking thing down. This is not going to work, Preecha. I love it but it takes too long. Take it back up and see how fast it can go without the wobble."

Over the next hour, Barry feeds programming orders to Preecha: "Syncros, add strobes, explosion! Then full lights, laser shooting through, all samurai on, pin spots, two times outer chase. . . Slow roll circle. Nah, I don't like it. Let's see all red. . . . No, not the red. Back to all slow roll, I'm starting to like it."

As Preecha goes through the programming cues, John Goss sits by the Phantom laser projector, reading *Interview with a*

Vampire. "This is like the army," he observes. "Hurry up and wait."

A serious glitch occurs when the Show/CAD program keeps overriding the Phantom laser. The technicians keep trying and failing to link lights and lasers.

"This software is no good," Preecha tells Barry.

"It sucks, as we say in New York."

Ponlawat Sookcharus, A.V. Systems managing director, arrives to see how things are going. "When will the show be ready?" he asks Barry.

"About the year 2000. We're going to have to pay someone from the outside."

○

That someone is Mark McKibben, a burly, bushy-bearded lighting consultant from Los Angeles.

But on February 1st, nine days before Opening Night, Barry reports, "Progress is going like a snail. I've brought in Mark, but the computers keep crashing. We've got 50 seconds programmed out of the five-minute Terminator show, and that's just one of four. The problem is the Show/CAD software just can't save cues."

"Or sometimes you can save," Mark McKibben observes wearily. "Just enough to give you false hope."

"We waste whole days identifying a computer problem when we should be being creative. There's no problem with the hardware. The Show/CAD software is the computer from hell."

"There are only 200 of these animals in the world," adds John Willemse. "We got the program from Coma, an Australian company, but the manufacturer is in London. And they don't have a programmer they can send to us."

Barry gets on his mobile phone to the A.V. Systems secretary. "Monica, call London right now. Tell Mick Martin he *has* to talk to me. I'm the customer, he's the software manufacturer. And I've got to be able to reach London whenever I need them. Australia doesn't know what the hell they're doing."

Mark stands up from the computer, stretches, lights a cigarette. There are cigarette butts all over the floor: Barry's Parliaments, John's Dunhills.

"The problem is memory allocation," Mark complains. "Show/CAD can't handle a system this big." He looks at the cigarette in his hand. "I don't normally smoke. But I do here. Many things you can say about Bangkok, but it's never dull."

Barry is on the phone to London. "Look, I've got 1,200 lights to coordinate and it has to be ready by the end of next week. Your system—patch, copy, save, file—could have been easier. . . . Look, I've got a modem in my hotel and we'll fax you a printed out program: the whole program and subdivisions, program file, back up, all printed, config file, Show/Cad config. Can you use compu-serve. . . ? You get the advantages of e-mail then. . . . Okay, okay."

Barry puts the phone down. "Was I polite? The New York didn't come out, did it?" He lights another cigarette. "They're sending us a third version which *might* work. We're on version two now."

Barry takes over the computer to add a few more seconds of programming on SMPTE. John Willemse keys in the lasers for the final dry run of the night. The sound effects of *Terminator* boom as the center disc, shooting out strobes in time, descends from the ceiling.

"STOP! STOP! CUT!" Barry yells. "Piece of shit! What the hell is this?" He peers at his computer: "*Fail security test*? All right, let's move all that crap again."

On the second try, all eight sections split, rear up and descend at varying angles, blazing in time around the center disc. The effect is spooky, dazzling, spectacular. Barry lowers the whole rig to the floor for bulb changes. He leans back in his chair. "We made progress today. We added a few more seconds."

As they pack up to go, Mark explains how he got into the lighting game. "I was in medical school and I figured if I was going to stay up all night I'd rather do something entertaining. So I got my MA at UCLA in Theater Arts. Did lighting for Kenny Rogers, John Denver, moved to industrial and TV work, CBS for a while. I like switching around, looking for new fields. When Barry called me for this job, I had to come here."

"Why? For the challenge?"

Mark rolls his eyes in exasperation. "Obviously!"

○

Four days later, Barry's voice is groggy on the phone: "We still can't get it to work. We're in touch on e-mail with the manufacturer in London. We keep downloading new stuff and the computer keeps crashing. We're working late every night. And we're running out of time!"

On February 9th, the eve of Opening Night, John Willemse is, frankly, glum.

Someone asks him how things are going. "They're not," John says. "Barry shot Mark at four this morning, then committed suicide at six."

The name of the London company is Axon Digital Communications and Barry has told them that the job is beyond what they can do. He is rewriting the whole configuration. "Basically, Barry is teaching *them* now," John explains. "He's reconfiguring the program which isn't even known as Show/CAD now but Beta 211–23. Officially it's a test, not ready for release."

Barry and Mark slump into the control booth. Both look haggard.

"That 50-second bit that we'd recorded before has been lost," Barry grumbles. "*Program deleted*! I'm supposed to be a lighting designer, not a computer fixer. I was on the phone till four-thirty this morning, another phone call at nine-thirty and back to work. Mark's spent the last eight hours logging cues. I'm getting out of this game. Only thing I'll come back to Thailand for is the food. Pol Pot had the right idea: get rid of Western technology."

John nods in agreement. "Freds," he mutters.

"Freds?"

"It's a trade term: Fucking Ridiculous Electronic Devices."

"What we have to do now," Barry says, "is program the mini-keyboard so I can wing it tomorrow night. I asked Mick Martin if he'd programmed for mini-keyboard. No. Asked him if he owned a mini-keyboard. No. Told him to buy one. And now my mobile phone has conked out, so I'm cut off from London. I've made more than my best effort. I'll wing it now, go home to New York, and I'll come back when they've got the software working."

Ponlawat comes in and is consulting with Barry and John when Mark rears back in horror from his computer screen—suddenly blank. "That's it! Crashed! I just lost 648 cues. Goddamn fucking mess!"

"Why am I not yelling and screaming?" Barry asks himself.

Mark plunges his face into his hands. "I feel like I'm in a bad episode of the Twilight Zone."

Ponlawat offers his mobile phone to Barry who gets right to the point with Mick Martin. "Why is this computer crashing? It crashed three times last night too. I've got level none, no access. Look, what I can do is get a new program that works. Or you send people here to program. . . So only you and your brother can do it? Both of you come. You'll *love* Bangkok . . ."

When Barry gets off the phone, he reports that Mick Martin is going into the hospital for oral surgery on Monday. "I'm giving up on Mick."

Two hours later, the computer has crashed twice more, but by 9:50 Barry announces that the mini-keyboard is loaded for a trial midnight show. The show goes off without a hitch. Barry and John decide to do an all-nighter to get ready for tomorrow's show, 22 hours away.

"How's it going?"

"It's going," John Willemse says. "We're getting there. Vast improvement."

○

At six in the evening, February 10th, a battalion of waiters are receiving last orders from a manager with a bullhorn. On the dance floor, to the pounding strains of *Terminator*, a dance troupe are going through rehearsal paces, strenuously lifting and spinning each other around. They will be accompanying the light show.

Barry and John have not slept for 32 hours. Mark came in from the hotel at 11 this morning. All have deep, raspy cigarette voices. Barry takes a half-hour break, leaving Mark to program in the last samurai lights. "I had to program from scratch," Barry says. "But things are looking up. I'm out of here on Tuesday. Northwest Airlines, first-class to New York."

At seven, a six-piece band in white jackets strike up a bossa nova number. Singers and dancers come and go. By nine, Phoebus is filling up with Bangkok's *jeunesse d'oro*, milling around the buffet tables. Shortly before ten, Charn Plantinon and the Phoebus board of directors line up on stage. From the control booth, a green laser streaks down to cut the ribbon. And the show is on!

The horns and drums of *Terminator* swell, and light panels rock, flash, whirl and hover down over the dance floor. Multi-colored ring lights spin, samurais dance, synchros march to the beat, and killer strobes stab the air—lasers beaming through the whole riotous phantasmagoria, rising higher and higher as *Terminator* reaches a mad percussive crescendo and. . . no one is looking up in awe at the light show. The female dancers are in flesh-colored body stockings. All eyes are on them.

A View from the Bridge

The Slum Dwellers

Every day, along Suksawat Road, thousands of drivers cross the bridge over Thonburi's Dao Kanong canal. Probably none of them are aware that hidden underneath it, a slum community of over forty families ekes out a meager living.

The bridge serves as the roof for a warren of fifty rooms, hammered together out of scrap wood and tin pan, and connected by meandering duck-boards, where women squat before wash basins and cooking pots; half-naked kids scamper about in the dirt; and mongrel dogs skulk around looking for scraps. Most of the dwellings are in perpetual gloom. Linoleum is spread over rough plank floors; furniture is a mattress and mosquito net; decoration is provided by torn-out magazine photos of Thai pop stars.

The south bank of the canal, or *klong*, was settled twenty years ago by two families from Ayuthaya. They were rice farmers escaping the devastation of floods, drought and failed crops. Later, they were joined by relatives and neighbors, and then by another contingent from Korat.

The Ayuthaya and Korat people intermarried, and soon formed the core of a tight-knit family community of 126 men, women and children. The men work as day laborers, carpenters, stevedores and junk collectors; and some of the women work in factories. Others pass the days tending small children, making paper flowers and jasmine garlands, and—that sure antidote to slum boredom—gambling with cards.

A few years ago—at the suggestion of Fr. Joe Maier and social workers of his Human Development Center—the community elected a leader, Chan Sigawpan. They began contributing 200 baht a month to a common fund, and launched the construction of a kindergarten.

The north bank of the *klong*—a mixed salad of 18 families from all over the Northeast—remains unorganized.

"They move in and out a lot, but we'll invite them to join the kindergarten," says Chan. "On our side of the *klong*, we're more stable. I settled here twenty years ago, following my older sister from Ayuthaya."

Chan's room is open to the *klong*, and he allows kids to crowd the floor, watching cartoons on TV. Laundry hangs from a line under the bridge. Chan's wife, Tongchua, tends the slum's sole shop, selling soft drinks and *lao kao* (rice whiskey moonshine). In a place where people earn an average of 100 baht a day, purchases tend to be small: a single cigarette, two candles, one-baht candy.

Beyond the shop, the open space between the bridge's two carriageways makes for a natural skylight. A few benches and wooden platforms serve as a community gathering place. Chan proudly shows off the pile of lumber and tin pan, donated by the Human Development Center, which the carpenters in the slum will transform into a one-room kindergarten.

"We need the kindergarten," says Chan's daughter, Kanchalee. "Living over the water is dangerous for little kids. Their mothers can't be watching over them all the time. Also, the kindergarten will free some of the mothers to find work outside."

Kanchalee, 18, is the mother of a five-month-old boy. She used to work on construction projects, but is supported now on the monthly 3,000 baht her husband makes as a mechanic. Bright-eyed and articulate, she graduated from junior high school—a scholastic achievement in a community where few have completed primary school.

"The kids here go to a nearby temple school," she continues. "But there's a problem for those who don't have house registration papers. Most people have their home province papers, but for kids who don't, they can't go to school. Our immediate problem now is water. With the flood on the Chao Praya, the government has closed the *klong's* watergates. We used to use the canal water for bathing and washing clothes, but now it's turned black and smelly. Even when it flowed freely, the water was brackish and made people itchy. We get no help from the government. Politicians come and go, but none of them care about the poor."

The slum dwellers are squatters on land that is owned by the Department of Irrigation. They are worried that they will be evicted if the government goes ahead with plans to tear down the bridge and build a new one.

"That's why we're putting money in the bank—so we can all move to a new place together," explains Chan. "The problem is where?"

"We don't want to move far from here," adds Lui Gannambat, another long-term resident, who moved from another nearby bridge slum, Sapan Nakhon. "I know this area well. I've got a bicycle cart and collect junk. But if we move far from here, how can I make a living?"

Lui averages 100 baht a day. His neighbor, Lek Lamool, earns 150 baht in a toy factory.

"I came here a year ago from Mahasarakam," she explains. "Life's not good here, but at home there's nothing. I left to find money. My husband is still looking for work. Our two youngest kids are with my mother in Mahasarakam, but we manage to keep the eldest in school here."

Another community leader is Chumphon Sonsam, a carpenter who came to the slum from Prachinburi 14 years ago. He will lead the men in constructing the kindergarten, once the floodwaters go down. His room boasts a fridge, a stereo and a television, and—open to the main gathering place—it forms a center for the community.

"I sent my money back to Prachinburi for my children's education," he says proudly. "My daughter is in the civil service now; my two sons in the police and the army."

Chumphon's natural leadership is put to the test three days later—a hot Saturday—when the slum is crowded with people off from work. The men are drinking heavily, the women are gambling, and some are doing both. The men are lean, muscular and tattooed. The women are heavily-built, their easy smiles marred by missing teeth. All smoke cigarettes and some chew betel nut. They dominate a circle of gamblers by the *klong* bank.

Two men suddenly break into a fistfight over the twenty baht pot. In a flash, everyone is up on their feet, cursing, shouting, shoving, breaking into smaller fights, or trying to restrain others. A huge woman nearly manages to make peace, but the uproar explodes again, spilling out into the slum's center. One man, very drunk, squares off into a Thai boxing stance. His opponent, not so drunk, lays into him with punches and kicks. The drunk reels backwards, blood spurting from his mouth.

Chumphon wades in between them. "You're out of control!" he shouts to the drunk, and punches him in the face. As the second man is still spoiling for a fight, Chumphon punches him too. The man responds with a *wai*, and the fight fizzles out.

Earlier, Chan had boasted that there was no drug-taking in his slum and no thievery—"Everyone here knows each other."— but he is deeply embarrassed now.

"Do fights like this happen a lot?" I ask.

He shakes his head in disgust and says nothing.

There Goes the Neighborhood

The Slum Activists

For a slum, Ban Krua can be downright pretty. Off the main roads lined with ugly concrete shophouses, down along *Klong* Saen Saeb, here you will find a quieter, gentler, more harmonious Bangkok. A Bangkok of old shade trees and wooden houses with flowerpots that hang from rattan-furnished porches, and shuttered windows that open on four sides to the wind. It is no coincidence that perhaps the most beautiful home in Bangkok—Jim Thompson's House—is located in Ban Krua. The people here were the traditional weavers upon which the legendary American built his silk empire.

Ban Krua is a 200-year-old community of Muslim Chams from Cambodia, who were settled in Bangkok by King Rama I in recognition of their loyal military service to Siam. A century later, when French gunboats advanced up the Chao Praya during the reign of Rama V, Muslim sailors fought fiercely for Siamese independence. Half of them were killed and are buried in Ban Krua's three Muslim cemeteries.

In 1987, a very different threat loomed: a cemetery and a mosque were targeted for destruction by the Expressway and Rapid Transport Authority (ETA) to make way for the Bang Khlo-Chaeng Wattana Expressway. Ban Krua residents protested, saved the mosque, and launched a seven-year battle to preserve their community from continuing threats from developers.

As the years wore on, the 700 families of Ban Krua became increasingly savvy in fighting City Hall. A neighborhood community was organized and elected a forty-year-old Bangkok Electricity Authority worker, Saroj Pueksamlee, as president. The community now spoke with one voice. Later, Suvit Watnoo became an adviser to Saroj. As director of the Human Settlement Foundation—an NGO devoted to slum-dweller rights—Suvit was a veteran of many eviction battles.

The Ban Krua committee forced a series of public hearings on the expressway project. This allowed the community to put its case to the media. Three hundred and twenty families were threatened with eviction so that a 2,000 meter approach ramp—four times longer than normal—could service the commercial interests of the World Trade Center area.

In September 1993, the government committee came down on the side of the Ban Krua residents, recommending that the approach ramp be scrapped. Seven months later, in a surprise move, the ETA went ahead with its eviction order. Slum activists—and newspaper editorials—accused then ETA Governor Sukhavich Rangsitphol of a cozy relationship with the Techapaibul family, owners of the World Trade Center.

The Ban Krua committee sent a protest letter to Prime Minister Chuan Leekpai, and staged a public rally before Government House. The rally displayed a masterful media touch. Demonstrators captured front-page newspaper photos as they dug graves in Muslim cemeteries in preparation for the first martyr deaths. Student and Muslim associations rallied in support. Before Government House, an orderly crowd of 300, dressed in traditional religious garb, held prayer sessions. Under banners petitioning justice, elderly residents in wheelchairs held up portraits of the royal family.

The government capitulated. As the demonstrators dispersed peacefully, Prime Minister Chuan came out to shake hands with community leaders. Photo posters of this meeting were quickly plastered on the walls of Ban Krua homes and shops.

"Those were good tactics," recalls a smiling Suvit Watnoo in his office of the Human Settlement Foundation. "By demanding public hearings, the Ban Krua community was saying, 'We are *not* a colony with no voice or right to be heard.'

My organization's specialty is to advise on tactics. My staff of ten includes a media adviser, a lawyer, and an accountant. We focus on land-use and housing issues, compiling data, and offering advice to neighborhood committees.

"The difference between now and ten years ago is that slum communities are now organized. The Bangkok Metropolitan Authority estimates 1,232 slum communities in the capital, and 1,840 nationwide in regional centers like Chiang Mai, Korat, Saraburi, Songkhla and Hat Yai. Every year in Bangkok between 15,000 and 20,000 people face eviction. Thirty percent have received some aid from NGOs. We can offer a methodology for upgrading and reconstruction of slums, and also organize savings groups so squatters can buy the land they occupy."

After graduating with a degree in education from Ban Saen's Srinakarinwirot University, Suvit taught for two years in Rayong, and then moved to Chumphon to organize cooperatives for coffee and oil palm growers. Eight years later, he began working for the Duang Prateep Foundation—which trains and organizes community leaders—in Bangkok's biggest slum, Klong Toey. Six years of experience in Klong Toey led him to set up the Human Settlement Foundation in 1991.

Klong Toey is the grandfather of all Bangkok slums, the training ground for a whole generation of community organizers. After 1945, the slum sprang up on vacant land owned by the Port Authority of Thailand (PAT). It was a mutually beneficial relationship: dock workers needed housing and the PAT needed dock workers. The community swiftly grew to 25,000, but the crunch came in 1970 when the PAT needed more land for port expansion and began wholesale evictions. Squatter families resisted and their homes were simply bulldozed.

Klong Toey responded by organizing a community committee at the "one-baht-a-day" school of Prateep Ung-songdham. Prominent academics lent support to the slum dwellers, and the committee mustered the bargaining power to deal with the PAT.

The community movement gathered steam during the 1973–1976 period of full-fledged democracy, culminating in the establishment of the National Housing Authority (NHA), a government organization dedicated to building low-income housing and upgrading existing slums.

In 1978, Prateep Ungsongdham received the Magsaysay Award for her community service and promptly donated her prize money to form the Duang Prateep Foundation. Klong Toey was ready for the next round of battles in 1982 when its committee negotiated a land-sharing agreement with the PAT. The era of wholesale evictions was over.

Another prominent NGO working in support of Klong Toey's survival has been the Human Development Center, founded by Fr. Joe Maier—an American priest who has lived in Klong Toey since 1966. Organization techniques pioneered in Klong Toey have since been transferred to other slums throughout the city.

"What we can do is to prepare people to face the challenge of eviction," Fr. Maier explains. "Violence doesn't work. You have to get people to have a position on the land in order to start positive negotiations. Possession is nine tenths of the law. Fires are common in slum areas, and if people lose their houses—if they're just sitting on the roadside like sick dogs—they have no negotiating power. For example, there was a fire at a slum called Sua Yai on Asoke Road. Twenty-four houses were destroyed, so we trucked in wood and tin roofing so people could throw up shelters immediately—and demonstrate their intent to stay. Fortunately, the fire broke out before a four-day holiday weekend, so they re-established their presence on the land before the owner, the Irrigation

Department, had time to act. The district officer set up a sign saying construction was illegal for 45 days after the fire. But once he'd performed his duty, he didn't care.

"The police won't bother you unless somebody has hired them to do it," Fr. Maier adds. "However, if you have the district officer, the police *and* the landlord wanting you off the land, that's the real witches' brew. On that occasion, they didn't get there in time. The wheels of government move slowly and ponderously, and a quickstepping NGO can keep one jump ahead of the process. You can stall for negotiations for four or five years."

The master strategist in land-use negotiations is Somsook Boonyabancha of the Urban Community Development Office (UCDO). After gaining her architectural degree from Chulalongkorn University, she joined the National Housing Authority in 1977.

"The first job I had was to design a community center for Ban Krua," Somsook recalls. "But just to draw up a design in an office is boring, so I went into the community to find out people's ideas on what they needed. The goal was to create a design that people fitted into comfortably. Soon, I was deeply involved with community committees and NGOs in trying to solve the problems of land-use and evictions.

"In 1982, I made a pilot study and found that 25% of all slum dwellers were living under the threat of eviction. The idea was to forecast which areas would be affected, where to intervene, and what constructive approaches to use. I negotiated with the landlords of Sam Yod and Wat Lad Bua Kaw. Squatters had been on their land for decades, but the landlords reasoned that they had the right to evict them.

"The Thai way of avoiding conflict is to share the land— part for low income housing, part for commercial development. Four hundred families in one slum, for example, were offered land at one quarter of the market price, and were then helped with long-term NHA loans.

"I'd estimate that 10% of Bangkok's slums are well-organized, and another 20–30% have some form of organization. When people resist, the system recognizes them. This is crucial to the next step of negotiations: either compensation or land-sharing. The paramount issue is security. Squatters and renters need to know that any physical improvements they organize—concrete walkways, drainage, water supply, garbage collection, day care centers—will be part of a permanent community.

"At one time, the government's idea was that slums were temporary structures, destined for eventual demolishment. Their perception has changed. The government now wants to upgrade communities that are permanent and secure."

Somsook left the NHA to join the UCDO at its founding in June 1992. Bringing together the government, the private sector, NGOs and community committees, the UCDO offers low interest loans to slum dwellers who decide to stay in place and buy their own land, rather than accept compensation for moving out.

"Meanwhile, slum communities are raising their own funds through savings groups," says Somsook. "I estimate that 300 urban groups have raised between 200–300 million baht in funds. We can assist this process—and so work less. As it is now, the UCDO funds its operations and its staff of eighty through a loan interest rate that averages out to 8%. The bankers in our group would like to raise that rate for more profitability; the community leaders to lower it. It's a never-ending fight. But it's better to fight in the boardroom than on the street," Somsook concludes with a laugh.

One who could not agree more is slum activist, Sompong Patpui. After twenty years of organizing people to fight City Hall, Sompong now *is* City Hall. Chairman for Community Development in Governor Bhichit Rattakul's Bangkok Metropolitan Administration (BMA), his mandate is Bangkok's vast network of slums—home to a fifth of the city's population.

Since taking office in June 1996, Sompong has been orchestrating innovative housing and social action programs—with input from slum dwellers themselves.

What to do, for example, about the squatter communities that live under 83 of Bangkok's bridges?

"We have two priorities," Sompong replies at his second floor office at City Hall. "One is to maintain the bridges, check the structures, and make repairs. Second, we have to improve the living environment of the people. You have problems with drugs, with children's health, and with the general quality of life. This is not just a housing problem, but a human development problem—and a long-term one.

"I meet with elected slum leaders and NGOs, and together with the BMA and the NHA (National Housing Authority), we're searching for land to resettle the bridge communities. We've established three relocation zones in Bangkok. The important thing is that the new housing can't be too far away from their original sites because that's where they earn their living. This isn't a big number we're talking about—only 2,000 people—and they should all be moved out in a year or so. A second problem, of course, is that once they've moved out from under the bridges, how do you stop other people from moving in to replace them? The BMA is committed not to exercise police violence in evicting people. We have to provide alternatives.

"Most slums have *prachakom*—community committees—with leaders elected for a term of two years. They're registered with the BMA and accepted by us to represent their neighborhoods. But they haven't been given much support in the past. The BMA preferred to work from the top down. The *prachakom* had no budget and found it difficult to contact officials. Our policy now is to actively promote the community committees. We want to combine them into greater committees citywide with representatives elected to a higher council to advise the governor."

Sompong estimates that 1,000 neighborhood groups, with an average of 250 families in each, are ready to join the large committees. Many were organized by urban NGOs, but others sprang up independently.

"There are 15 strong areas in Bangkok like Klong Toey and Ban Krua," he notes. "Many others will become stronger if the government supports them. I've been to ten areas to meet with neighborhood leaders and to encourage them to design a community plan. I'll give you an example. In Kon Tiem district, I met with 29 neighborhood associations: with health care volunteers, youth groups, people running day care centers and campaigns against drugs. There are 200,000 people in that district and they're eager to form a *prachakom* Kon Tiem and to create a district plan. They have common problems: clear-cut issues like floods, toxic waste, muddy roads, environmental concerns, and drugs.

"We're devising a five-year plan for Bangkok, and I want to integrate into it *prachakom* community plans for each of Bangkok's forty districts: social issues, housing, sanitation. The community committee will draw up a plan and a budget, and the BMA will consider it and then release funds. We have money for anti-drug projects. Again, the communities will have control of the budget. We're decentralizing power. This is totally new."

Sompong came to his slum work in a roundabout way. He grew up on his father's forty-*rai* rice farm in Pathum Thani, attended high school in Nonthaburi, and then joined the Royal Thai Navy. For ten years, he served as a torpedo man at the navy's Bangna ordnance base, attending night school until he was able to pass the entrance examination for Chulalongkorn University. He graduated in 1973 with a degree in accountancy, and went straight to work for Bangkok Metropolitan Bank in Klong Toey.

"I worked for the bank for three years," he recalls. "But I was bored with the job and found social work in the Klong

Toey slum more exciting. At that time Prateep [Ungsongdham Hata] was just starting her illegal 'one-baht-a-day' school. I helped run the school, set up youth groups, organized people to protest against evictions, and set up a community council of slums—which we expanded to 13 areas outside Klong Toey. Those were exciting times—better than being dead."

With the military crackdown of October 1976, Sompong was forced to flee to the jungle and the hospitality of the Communist Party of Thailand. He came out of the jungle in 1979, a year after Prateep had won the Magsaysay award and established her Duang Prateep Foundation. Sompong returned to work there as deputy director. In 1990, he established his own NGO—the Grassroots Development Institute.

So, after two decades of grassroots organization, how did he wind up in City Hall?

"I moved into politics with Khun Bhichit [Rattakul]. I've known him for ten years, since when he was an MP from Klong Toey. I made suggestions how to get the vote out from the slums. He was very active. He saw ways to solve problems with a new approach; a new vision. I joined him in his campaign for BMA governor. The election was a success, and afterward Khun Bhichit asked me what I wanted to do.

"Social issues are tough, and getting worse. In terms of infrastructure for social development, there's nothing. Four years from now, I hope to have set up a structure that can sustain social development. Our policy is to decentralize power to the forty districts. Social development work will be taken care of by elected committees in each district. We have to develop a community-based approach. If people don't agree, if they're not in a strong organization, they can't do anything. But if people succeed in one thing, they'll expand to another. First they might set up a kindergarten, then build walkways, then form youth groups, then move into an anti-drugs program. Action will come from people themselves.

Take drugs, for example. Before, the approach was from the top down—police simply arrested drug users. But an integrated community approach—from the bottom up—is a much better way to rid a neighborhood of drugs."

Looking around the region, Sompong cites other cities—Bombay, Karachi and Manila—which have strong slum organizations. They are not, however, integrated into the city government, as he envisions the Bangkok community committees to be. A greater council representing Bangkok's forty districts will have an institutional voice with the BMA governor.

How does he view his progress?

"Well, I spent the early months getting to know the car and how to repair it," he replies. "I moved up to first gear, slow and clumsy. Then second gear. Maybe by the end of my term I'll be in fifth gear and going fast. Or I'll roll right off the road. I'd also like to know more about the road," he concludes with a laugh. "And what's beside the road."

The Good, the Bad, and the Ugly

The Architects

Americans like to say that Washington DC is a beautiful city with ugly buildings, and New York is an ugly city with beautiful buildings.

If that is true, what is Bangkok?

The whole history of architecture—an insane jumble of everything from the pharaohs and the Greeks, to cut-rate copies of Gothic and Pop architecture. The construction boom of the eighties and early nineties had a disastrous effect upon the city skyline—leaving a bizarre mix of the good, the bad, and the very ugly. But with the collapse of the building boom, there is cautious optimism—especially among members of the Association of Siamese Architects (ASA)—that the cityscape will become a kinder, greener one.

On April 18th, 1933, the founders of ASA numbered under forty. By 1965, when the reigning generation of Thai architects—Dr. Sumet Jumsai Na Ayudhya, Dan Wongprasat, Chuchawal Pringpuangkeo, Ong-Art Satarapandu, Rangsan Tawsuan and Nithi Sthapitanonda—were graduating from university, membership stood at 400. Today, that number is 4,000 and climbing. The explosive growth of ASA mirrors Bangkok's own.

ASA's founding members were educated overseas, mainly in Great Britain. In 1934, Thailand's first architectural school was opened at Chulalongkorn University, but nowadays architects graduate from Silapakorn, Sukhothai, Rangsit and Lard Krabang, as well as provincial universities in Hat Yai and Khon Kaen. Since the sixties, American universities have

replaced British as the institutions of choice for overseas education. By the mid-eighties, enough architects were in place to handle the Bangkok building boom. Probably a few too many. The boom years saw the wanton destruction of many historical buildings to make way for new developments.

Dan Wongprasat regrets the demolition of much priceless architecture. He and Dr. Sumet Jumsai, among others, have chaired the ASA's Art and Architecture Preservation Committee, which inventories national heritage buildings across the country and launches publicity campaigns for architectural preservation. "We have the first information about demolition plans and can apply pressure," declares Dan. "Sometimes we win, sometimes not."

Of equal concern to him is the quality of modern architecture. "Construction went on too fast, and now we're stuck with ugly buildings. With the building boom came a craving for big-scale construction. Younger architects were eager to make their name and they'd take low fees just to get the chance to throw up a forty-story building. But they had no experience and paid no attention to details—leaving that to contractors. They lost contact with their culture through cut-throat economic competition. It's very sad. You either know architecture or you don't. Books and schools can't tell you everything. You have to come to terms with your *karma* and your nationality.

"In Bangkok nothing was generated from Thai values. Big glass boxes are the worst thing that happened to this city. The need is to build from an Asian Buddhist base—to build upon what we have. Architecture should be historically related to our past. Consistent. I don't mean temple style with all the mosaic, but a feel for our historical background— a continuity to develop into the future.

"I built the Regent Hotel according to Buddhist architectural motifs. There's a reflecting pool at the entrance, symbolizing passage into spiritual life. The principle was to keep the Regent simple—nothing fancy. The idea was a group of Thai houses with many levels and courtyards, as well as gardens and watercourses, and paintings and landscaping. It's like composing a symphony. There has to be a harmony in the spaces. I consider the Regent my masterwork. I was given a completely free hand and I was happy. There were no changes until completion.

"I haven't always had such good clients. After working for two years on the Peninsula Hotel, I lost the job after I insisted on keeping it lower than the owners wanted. I designed a hotel in Mae Hong Son but have yet to be paid my fee. The big architectural companies avoid getting stiff-armed by demanding 10% up front, but small architects are not always such good businessmen. I've kept my staff small—15 assistants—because I prefer to work on just one or two projects at a time."

Asked to name some of the really bad buildings in Bangkok, Dan throws up his hands and laughs. "So many! Including mine! Once the job is done, you see your mistakes. But the international glass boxes and the Japanese style predominate in Bangkok. I prefer an architecture that is more subtle and romantic. I find Pop architecture offensive: multi-colored, odd shapes. I tell my students at Chulalongkorn to beware of fads. Nowadays there are so many trendy architectural magazines—as many as for fashion and interior design. Thailand is crazy about these things. But the thing is, architecture is not about fashion, but about human needs. I tell my students to remember the basic things. Like a spoon: you have a handle because you have a hand, and the scoop to pick things up with.

"Architecture is 3-D art, up and down and in and out—the relationship between inside and outside. People are beginning to understand this now, and I do think the younger generation has produced nicer architecture in recent years."

A large photo of the Regent hangs in Dan's studio, and a hand-printed message below it sums up his philosophy. *"The essence of present-day Thai architecture is . . . to be able to look at, and understand the meaning of the past with pride; to be able to look to the future with this all-important sense of cultural constancy without the complication of being tangled in the hierarchy of being avant garde or hors concours."*

In contrast to a small-scale individualist like Dan Wong-prasat is an architect-as-developer, Chuchawal Pringpuang-keo. Twenty-five years ago, when he returned to Bangkok from New York's Pratt Institute, Chuchawal began as an architectural firm of one, designing his father's home and a small Volvo showroom on Soi Asoke.

Today, he employs 250 architects, engineers, landscapers and construction technicians. His three companies—Design 103 Ltd., Chuchawal-De Weber International, and Thai Project Management Co.—occupy several floors of Asoke Towers, a project of his own design.

From his eighth-floor headquarters, Chuchawal points out another of his creations—the National Housing Board Building, a graceful white triangular building dwarfed by boxy behemoths of reflecting glass. "In a tropical country, you have to deal with the heat," he observes. "Now, my building is pleasing to look at, and practical as well. Its three faces deflect rather than reflect the sun. That other building next to it faces east-west, and in the morning and afternoon becomes very hot, confronting the sun at a ninety-degree angle. My building conserves energy, since the three sides are positioned not to present themselves directly toward the sunlight. The three facades are all different, yet they fit together. The other big glass boxes don't mean anything. North, east, west, south—they all look the same.

"In good architecture you see three things: when? where? and with what technology? You see an ancient Greek building and you know where it came from, when it was built, and with what technology—in its case, stone. European and American buildings fit their locations. The architecture of Bangkok should be adapted to the climate, the Thai people, and the environment. In contrast, that glass box opposite reflects blinding sunlight into my office."

Over a quarter century, Chuchawal has designed such landmarks as the Central Bank of Thailand, the Boonrawd Brewery Headquarters, the Singha Bier Haus, the Hilton Intercontinental, the Landmark Hotel, and—his crowning achievement—the Queen Sirikit National Convention Center. The Center has won widespread praise for its combination of Thai design and high-technology.

"Traditional Thai architecture used terracotta roofs with a gap for insulation and an overhang for natural ventilation. I designed the Queen Sirikit Convention Center with these traditions in mind. The open spaces where people are passing through are provided with natural light. This generates heat, of course, so computer-programmed curtains close automatically at certain times of the day to reduce energy loss.

"Excellent new technologies are available in architecture now. Thirty years ago, Bangkok was just monotonous rows of shophouses. That was the format that generated the quickest economic return. With the boom there were opportunities for creativity, but architects weren't careful enough and often just made the cityscape worse. There was more work but not enough quality. An example of this is the Laksi Plaza. Tourists leave Don Muang airport and see this huge complex with no hint of Thai culture or way of life. A facade. I admire the Regent Hotel for its intelligent design, and the Sukhothai—not the exterior so much, but the interior is rich with cultural background."

In getting to the nub of what separates good architecture from bad, Chuchawal contrasts the Oriental and the Sheraton hotels. "Look at the Oriental. It has a well-designed ground floor next to the river. It's a relaxing, big space; dignified and comfortable. In the Sheraton you don't get the impression of being next to the river. It's badly positioned. The architect didn't realize how important the river is to people in Bangkok. Good Thai architecture shows an appreciation of the environment. You don't feel relaxed in the Sheraton. You do, totally, in the Oriental.

"What's needed are more buildings with the cityscape in mind: plazas, parks, trees and gardens. Freshness in the middle of the city. A good example is the Queen's Park on Sukhumvit Road, and people should thank Major-General Chamlong for it. They should also thank Santi Bhirombhakdi of Boonrawd, who sacrificed ten million baht of land for landscaping of the Singha Bier Haus, providing a patch of green on Soi Asoke."

Like Dan Wongprasat, Chuchawal is dismissive of the new Pop architecture.

"Architecture should reflect what's happening inside; the character of the building must be expressed outside. There should be a whole effect. I take buildings on a case by case basis and don't stick to one mold. If you're building a house, it's very important to know who lives in that house. I spend many, many hours with clients learning their habits, their daily schedules, their likes and dislikes. The idea is to build the house from the inside out. If a person spends a lot of time in the bathroom, make it big. The living room will be shaped according to the family's lifestyle. Are they private or do they like to entertain? Do they share the same tastes in TV or videos? If the wife likes soap operas, build the husband a den or a study. Call it what you like," Chuchawal laughs, "but that's where he can slip off to watch sports in private."

A former employee of Chuchawal is Nithi Sthapitanonda. After taking his MA in architecture from the University of Illinois, Nithi worked for Chuchawal for 12 years before launching his own firm—Architects 49 Ltd.—in 1983. After a single decade, his staff grew from five to 400. Among his projects are the Chao Praya Wing of the Shangri-La Hotel, the Holiday Inn in Chiang Mai, the Petroleum Authority of Thailand Headquarters, and the Lake Rajada Office Condominium.

Nithi, a former president of ASA, explains its functions. "We hold monthly meetings and seminars, and once a year we award gold medals to outstanding designs in four categories: Thai architecture, general architecture, preservation, and experimental design. We also present awards to the owners of buildings who preserve sites of historical and artistic value. Whenever we learn of a threatened building, we launch a preservation campaign and try to get the building listed on the Fine Arts Department's Register of National Heritage Sites.

"On the whole, I'd characterize the 4,000 architects of the ASA as well-educated, hard-working with a good attitude toward their trade, and attentive to both the environment and a building's impact on people. Some, of course, are interested only in money. The building boom happened too fast. There was no time for preparation and proper planning; no emphasis on the environment. Architects just followed the needs and demands of developers. There were big projects but nothing of value. Lately, though, architects are doing work that's better in many ways, with plazas, landscaping, atriums, wiser use of space, better planning, and improved finishing and use of materials. Granite has been adapted to high-rise uses, and aluminum is now easier to use since import taxes have been reduced."

Nithi lists his favorite buildings in Bangkok as the Regent, the Diethelm Towers, the Siam Intercontinenal, the Hilton Hotel, and the Thai Military Bank.

And the worst buildings?

"Too many!" he laughs. "But at least now, a law has been passed which mandates that six meters around all sides of a building site be set aside for landscaping.

"Some recent buildings draw attention to the ego of the architect. This is a matter of taste, but it doesn't fit with my kind of designs. I think first in terms of function, and I talk a long time with my clients about their needs. As for looks, I like to simplify. I pay attention to details and materials, and also provide for gardens, fountains, sculpture and art; the complete picture—to make sure that the building fits into the environment. It takes a long time and a lot of work. In general, I think architecture is improving. Most architects try to do a good job. They don't always prevail over greedy developers though."

Echoing these sentiments is Robert G. Boughey. "If you don't get a good client, you don't get a good building. Clients deserve the buildings they get."

A Pennsylvania native, Bob Boughey graduated from Pratt Institute in New York and worked for three years in Bangladesh as chief architect for Louis Berger Inc. He spent two years in Thailand, between 1964 and 1966, designing the National Indoor Stadium, and in 1970, returned with Louis Berger to work on such projects as the Siam Center. Four years later, he formed his own company—Robert G. Boughey & Associates—and went on to create such architectural gems as the Diethelm Towers, the Alma Link Building, the Bank of America Building, and the Siam Commercial Bank Park Plaza. His staff has since expanded from ten to forty.

"Some architects become developers," Boughey comments. "Others stay with a relatively small staff to produce quality architecture. The burden is on the owners to make buildings that are friendly to the environment. Things are somewhat better now. Before, there was no idea of a building's effect on a street. The idea was simply to use all the land up to the sidewalk. The perennial problem is finding good clients. There is still a hierarchical client/architect relationship. Architects, especially younger ones, are reluctant to push clients who might be insensitive and technically incompetent. Clients are polite to me, but some might ultimately say, 'Do what we tell you.' Which is a waste of money. And bad business besides.

"Eighty percent of the ugly buildings in Bangkok are the fault of developers. The new housing estates are horrible, with units all lined up in a row. You can look through one window and see through another fifty beyond. You see law suits filed now by tenants against owners for false promises.

"It's amazing how much construction went on during the boom. People bought shares in condos as a form of investment—like stocks—and had no intention of living in them. They never even looked at the plans. Developers were grabbing architects right after they left school. I hired one architect with six months experience who'd already built two thirty-story buildings. He decided to slow down and learn his trade."

Advised that all the architects interviewed for this story had expressed admiration for his Diethelm Towers, Bob Boughey responds with a smile. "It's popular. There are so many trees you can't see the building. I had a very good client who liked the land and intended to beautify it; and who had respect for the street. The American Embassy next door is happy with it. Each tower is angled at 45 degrees to the street, so two sides get the view. It's a logical solution. Angled this way, rather than frontally, there's less noise from the street too."

Like the Regent, the Diethelm Towers features landscaping that extends down to the sidewalk—without fencing to separate the gardens from the public.

"Clients are turning to better architects," Boughey continues. "Builders are giving back to the city, opening public space—which is only right. In the next building boom, I'd expect to see more trees and parks."

Boughey expresses admiration for the Regent and the Siam Intercontinental hotels, adding that, "I'm extending the Siam

THE GOOD, THE BAD, AND THE UGLY

Intercontinental and I hope not to ruin it. I like the Dusit Thani too. It's well planned with a distinct shape—Asian, if not Thai—and it fits nicely on its corner.

"Things go in cycles. Like the four or five huge condos and marinas that are opening on the riverside. The owners couldn't sell enough units so they've put their rich sons into them. Speedboats will be the next big thing. But I don't see rice barge captains giving way to these sporty new speedboats. I expect a lot of collisions on the river. A nice thing to watch, say, from the Oriental Hotel."

Architects on Architects

Architects are understandably reluctant to criticize the work of long-time friends and colleagues. The following are unattributed opinions about some of Bangkok's architectural landmarks:

The Asia Bank (Robot Building):

- "I like the Robot Building for its plaza. It's fun. Don't take it seriously."

- "The Robot Building doesn't mean anything. You design buildings not for personal fame but to house people. Are people comfortable in such buildings?"

The Baiyoke Tower:

- "The Baiyoke Tower is an example of Pop architecture, melding all shades of color. It's interesting but how do you repeat it? You don't want Bangkok looking like Disneyland."

- "The Baiyoke Tower is socially irresponsible—putting such a huge building on such a tiny *soi*. Its color scheme is lousy too."

- "The architect wanted Bangkok's tallest, flashiest building. But architecturally this is nothing special. The Thai are a colorful people so you throw up a lot of colors. A gimmick!"

The World Trade Center:

- "The World Trade Center is horrible. Unfriendly to pedestrians. A monolith with no windows. It isn't a place you want to stroll through. And it's the ugliest corner in town."

The Sheraton Hotel:

- "The worst box in Bangkok."

- "The Sheraton is horrible. Nobody likes it. The restaurant has no view."

The Ban Chang Glass Haus:

- "It looks great from the Sukhumvit side, but from Asoke you can see its ugly rear. If you're building a high-rise, you have to remember that people can see all sides."

The Nation Building:

- "The Nation looks like a Braque painting. Made with Lego blocks."

Reaching for the Sky

The Builders

Love it or hate it, there is no avoiding the Thai Wah Tower II on Sathorn Road. Whatever your opinion of the 61-story wafer-thin skyscraper, it is one of Bangkok's most striking buildings. In 1994, when the Thai Wah Tower was only 46 stories tall, I prowled through the guts of it.

○ ○ ○

In the vaulted concrete caverns of the unfinished tower, most of the workers are women, their faces wrapped in checkered scarves with straw hats pulled down over their heads like bonnets. Thawat Wichan, one of the 15 construction coordinators on site, confirmed that about 25% of the workers *were* women. "They work mainly on the lower levels doing plastering and finishing work," he tells me. "Men do the heavy labor on the top floors."

At the high-rise lift, Thawat stepped to the edge of the building and casually leaned over 12 stories of space to search for the cage. I hung back, tightening my grip on a beam as he chatted about the project. "The forty-sixth floor has just been completed. I expect the sixty-first to be topped-off five months down the line."

The cage arrived, crammed with hard-hatted workers, cement bags and iron rods. The senior quality surveyor of the project, Victor Smith, had mentioned earlier that, in Bangkok, these cages occasionally fell down due to shoddy maintenance. I squeezed my way in and resolutely did not look down. The cage zoomed upward and all of Bangkok was spread out on the horizon. At the top, the cage emptied and I noticed, to my horror, a two-and-a-half foot gap between

cage and building. Teetering on the edge, I was torn between looking where I put my foot—and down the 46-story abyss—or staring straight ahead and taking the biggest giant step of my life.

The giant step landed me safely.

The "roof" of the tower was a beehive of activity. Eighty workers were laying down a grid-work of rebars, hammering on wooden form-works, and manhandling into place floor slabs which dangled from the monster tower crane. The view was magnificent. Bangkok stretched to infinity, with the whole course of the Chao Praya in view from Banglamphu to the bend in the river at Klong Toey. I had previously thought that the greatest view of Bangkok was from the Dusit Thani's rooftop restaurant. From this dizzying height, the Dusit Thani was a toadstool.

Back on the ground, Thai Wah Tower II project director, CK Ho, hoisted up a large drawing of the tower and pointed to its greatest peculiarity: a four-story, open-air "sky window" on the fifty-first floor—designed to house a gym, lounge, sauna, Jacuzzis, and three eight-meter-tall palm trees.

"The idea is for businessmen to relax in the spa while getting an open-air sensation of Bangkok, especially at night. The building is so thin, I couldn't resist poking a hole in it," CK smiled. "You have to be a little mad sometimes. Actually, when the consultants did wind tunnel tests on a scale model, they found that the hole helped to relieve wind stress—serendipitously.

"Our design was dictated by the property site. BMA bylaws limit construction heights for a distance of 200 meters from Sathorn Road. So we drew up a half-and-half design. The front half of the building is 12 stories—a reception area and car park—and the back half is the 61-story tower: for offices up to halfway, and the Westin Hotel on the top thirty stories. The peculiarities of the site demanded that the tower be relatively thin. I call it 'an elephant on a pinhead.' We also positioned the three elevator cores to help stiffen the building against wind: a central core for the office floors, flanked by express and service lifts.

"The lines of the Thai Wah Tower II aren't massive, but thin and elegant, designed with clean, simple, good proportions. Even though it's three times the height of the first tower, both styles match to give the impression of a complex—the Thai Wah Plaza. Both have the same fluted corners, egg-crate patterns, and silver-grey and black glass motif—a case of the tail wagging the dog."

The German company Philip Holzmann was in charge of construction. According to Bob Kevorkian, managing director, the company employed 5,000 workers on ten major building sites. "We are proud to be associated with Thai Wah Tower II," he commented. "The building shows a lot of vision."

"The tower has unique engineering features too," added Chamlong Hongsuchon, vice president of the engineering consulting firm SEATEC. "The construction design called for a deep excavation for 15-meter steel pilings, and we use high-stress cement and a specially constructed pump and liquidizer to get the cement up to the high stories. Plasticizing chemical additives delay bonding. You don't want the cement drying too fast."

"This is one of the very few high-rise concrete buildings in the world made possible by advances in high-stress concrete," pointed out CK Ho. "In the US, Japan and Singapore, all high-rise buildings are made of steel. In Bangkok, though, steel is prohibitively expensive, while concrete is abundant. So we had to do the unorthodox and go with appropriate technology."

Another factor in the use of concrete was labor. In the US, where labor costs are high, steel is more economical. In Thailand the opposite is true. Labor is cheap, but skilled workers in steel are scarce.

Site engineer, Meta Teekakul, explained that, despite the challenges of building the tower, they were still working with a conservative design. But the idea was to allow the maximum use of space by reducing the thickness of columns and beams. Besides high-stress concrete, they used dense, reinforcing rods that are 40mm thick instead of the normal 28–32mm.

"A new technology I'm working with now is 'climbing form-work'—the first in Bangkok. Instead of the traditional method of assembling a cement form-work, then dismantling it, moving it about, and reassembling it, a climbing form-work rises on hydraulics. This saves a great deal of time."

Each specialist pointed out different factors that were of particular concern to him during the tower's construction.

A large part of Meta's job was installation work so that electrical lines could pass through beams. He made shop drawings of possible routes, and consulted with designers to see if the plans were feasible.

Drawings on paper are one thing, but could the plans be physically carried out on site? Meta also had to make sure that material was in stock, and to draw up plans for how many workers were needed for what type of job—the ideal being to fit the work force to the task, and not to have extra workers at extra cost.

Holzmann engineer George Smith reported that, as the lead contractor, the company had a workforce of 400 on site. Direct contractors—in charge of plumbing, electricity, air conditioning and lifts—accounted for another 200. A major task was coordinating each day's work, and the delivery of supplies. This called for daily meetings.

"The building site has limited access—a single lane—to Sathorn Road, which itself is often clogged with traffic jams," Smith pointed out.

"You can't have trucks backed up on Sathorn Road. You also have to rationalize the use of the building's two tower cranes. All the contractors made demands on their time, and the goal is to make the most economic use of them. It's a very complex job. Fortunately, we have excellent relations with the direct contractors. The ideal is to identify and antici- pate problems, and then work them out together—with the ultimate goal of getting the building completed on time and within budget."

Consultant Chamlong held meetings with contractors and designers to introduce client modifications, discuss problems, and plan long-term solutions. This meant maintaining good communication among the clients, architect, structural engineers, systems installers, and the lead contractor at Thai Wah.

"In the beginning there were tensions," he admitted. "The atmosphere among the various contractors was not so good. But now the various components of the building are working well together, although not without occasional problems."

Project manager Somsak Yingdeeyangyurn estimated that he spent 80–90% of his time scheduling cement deliveries. The trick, for him, was to order the right amount, with no excess. He also had to allow for the curfew on heavy traffic on Sathorn from 10 a.m. to 4 p.m. Deliveries normally started at 9 p.m., with concrete work going on until long after midnight.

The Thai Wah building comes equipped with expensive safety features not required by BMA regulations, including sprinkler systems, pressurized escape staircases, and eleva- tors programmed to descend to the ground at the first emer- gency.

"I'd expect there are unsafe buildings in Bangkok," said CK Ho. "I did research on high-rise fires and found that they happen quite often in South American cities like Sao Paulo. Shoddy construction. I've heard of provincial hotels in Thailand with dummy sprinkler heads. Builders put them in the ceiling to impress guests, but there is no water system behind them!"

While there are no such safety concerns about Thai Wah Tower II, the most amazing thing about the building is that, given its anorexic proportions, it does not simply blow over in the slightest breeze.

The View from the Top

A few years ago, if you glanced at the Bangkok skyline, you might have assumed that the national bird of Thailand was the construction crane, and that the birds were breeding like rats.

The two German Kroll cranes atop Thai Wah Tower II during its construction were capable of hoisting five tons. Most critical in their operation was the close teamwork between the operator and the rigger.

The crane rigger on a building site not only has to hook up the load, but also to balance and weigh it so there is no spin or fall. Loose material is an obvious hazard. Similarly, on freight platforms staggered throughout the height of the building—generally out of sight of the crane operator—the rigger must guide the placing of the load by walkie-talkie. The ideal is a smooth, delicate landing. If the load lands with a bang, not only are the materials damaged, but so is the platform, which is designed for only so much weight.

Given the cranes' exposure to high winds and heavy rains, safety is a major consideration. On the Thai Wah Tower, the cranes were checked on a daily and weekly basis by operators and maintenance technicians. More in-depth tests were performed every month, quarter, and year by independent specialists.

Cranes are protected from lightning by grounding cables. Close attention must always be paid to the wind, and careful planning is necessary for lifting bulky items like wall frames, which can easily get caught and twist in the wind. Early morning is the best time to hoist such items.

Given the stress of their job—alone and blind in a small, hot cabin—crane operators generally work no longer than six hours a day. They tend to be in their twenties and thirties.

"Their worst task," guessed Thai Wah engineer Victor Smith, "is climbing up that long ladder in the morning."

Operator Manoch Siddha, 25, from Kampaeng Phet, began work as a tower crane mechanic and advanced through on-the-job training to pass the company's operator test. His monthly salary when he worked on Thai Wah II was 10,000 baht.

"I work from seven in the morning till one in the afternoon," he said. "Then I switch off to another operator. It's a stressful job. Every load you lift is different. Eighty percent of my work is shifting material on the top level; 20% is hauling up supplies from the ground. You have to develop a sure touch on the hand levers. A gauge in the cab gives wind speed, but the direction you have to judge for yourself. There's also a warning horn. I haven't had an accident yet."

A few months later, Holzmann installed closed-circuit television in the crane cab—the first ever in Bangkok—and Manoch no longer had to work blind.

A Man in De-stress

The Journalist (Reporter's Notebook 3)

I am too fat. I drink too much. I smoke too much. As a big city journalist, the most exercise I ever do is stapling.

So I was a prime physical specimen for the stress-relief spa at the Westin Banyan Tree Hotel.

Two hours before my appointment at the Banyan Tree Spa, I awoke in my Banglamphu flophouse to discover that my glasses were missing. Legally blind, I groped through the rubble of my room—stacks of old magazines, dog-eared paperbacks, yellowing newspapers—growing steadily more frustrated and enraged.

One hour later: no glasses.

In a fury, I stomped out to the street and was nearly run over by a taxi. I told the driver instead to take me to the Thai Wah Tower II on Sathorn Road, home of the Banyan Tree.

The spa occupies the 51st to 54th floors. Inside the elevator, I found no button for the 51st floor, so punched the 50th instead. I stalked out into a hotel corridor and took the fire exit up one floor. This led to a broom closet.

Retracing my steps down to the 50th floor, I found the fire door locked behind me. I punched the door, marched downstairs, kicked the 49th floor door, and gave a savage pummeling to the 48th. The 47th opened and, eventually, jabbering obscenities, I bumbled my way up to the 53rd floor spa entrance lounge.

There, seated serenely on a sofa, were manager David Strubsole and assistant Alison Gibbs.

I stomped up to them, red-faced, pop-eyed, sweating, spitting, hyperventilating.

"I AM A PRIME CANDIDATE FOR STRESS THERAPY!" I explained.

Paul and Alison looked at me as if I were insane. Which I was.

They offered me water in a trendy stone cup, and suggested something called a *"lomi lomi* massage."

"An Indonesian massage—very light, very relaxing," Paul explained, backing away, making soothing gestures, as if I were a rabid grizzly.

An attendant led me down a spiral staircase to a locker room where I changed into bathrobe and slippers. Next came a hot shower and a spell in a sauna. Then I was led up to a massage room overlooking Lumpini Park, 52 floors below. I was beginning to take in my surroundings now: artwork, crystals, burning incense, gentle flute music in the air.

I was greeted with a *wai* by my masseuse. Her name was Noot, from Khon Kaen. She had been ten years in Bangkok, five as a masseuse at a beauty salon on Petchaburi Road. After further training by Alison Gibbs, she was a star at the Banyan Tree Spa.

"This is an Indonesian massage, right?" I asked

"No, from Hawaii."

"Hey, any port in a storm."

Noot had me face down on the massage bed, hands at my side, palms upward. My face fit into a hole in the bed which opened down to a bowl full of floating flowers. I felt a little silly, but was soon moaning with contentment as Noot poured aromatic oil on my back and began gently rubbing it into my stiff neck and shoulders. I gave out a deep shuddering sigh. My breathing and heartbeat slowed.

Noot shifted around to my head and, leaning over, rotated her sensuous hands down over shoulder muscles, biceps and palms, lower back. . . .

Stupefied, I drifted off into a fog. Time elongated in a haze of pleasure.

Noot moved down to my right leg, kneading and probing thigh and calf muscles, then the soles of my feet. I squirmed with delight. With childish anticipation, I waited for her to repeat the whole operation with my left leg.

"Does this hurt?" she asked.

"Mmmmmmmmmmmno."

It seemed like hours and hours passed. I was a limpid puddle of joy. Noot had me turn over on my back. Placing a black strip of cloth over my eyes, she rubbed more oil into my chest, throat, face. . . . I sighed and moaned.

And suddenly it was over.

Noot pulled the blindfold off and gestured for me to sit up. I didn't want to. I was bereft. I wanted her to massage me for a week. But no, I had to return to the real world. I shuffled, jelly-kneed, toward the door, and Noot propelled me forward by the hips. Then she led me down the spiral staircase, holding my arm like a nurse. I was a blissed-out invalid. At the locker room, she *wai*ed goodbye.

"Thankyouthankyouthankyou," I said.

After a while, I gathered my strength and wandered out to the skyview: the five-story-tall open area that soars 51 floors over a panoramic sweep of all Bangkok. Here, under a real banyan tree, I sampled the giant Jacuzzi, the turbo pool and the bubble lounge. I peered down at the Sukhothai Hotel—a mere mushroom in the shadow of Thai Wah II. I looked out for miles in the distance, to the port of Klong Toey, the ships anchored in the bend of the Chao Praya, and the gleaming span of the Rama IX Bridge. I reveled in the feeling of being on top of the world.

Only then did I remember that my glasses were gone.

Baa Baa Boh Boh
The Singer—Nanthida

Shopaholic, shoe fetishist, entrepreneur, Nanthida Kaew-buasai is one of Thailand's top singers. Her career began in 1978, when she beat out 549 other contestants to win a TV singing crown, and then went on to Hong Kong to compete against 15 vocalists from eight Asia-Pacific nations in the Third Asian Amateur Singing Contest. She blew the judges away with her rendition of "I Who Have Nothing." She was just 17.

Back in Thailand, Nanthida was invited to the annual Sports Day of the Stars, in which movie idols made fools of themselves at track and field events. Sponsor and sportswear tycoon, Suchada Nimakorn, invited the actors and actresses into her Grand Sport emporium to grab whatever equipment and clothing they needed. A businesswoman with no time for entertainment, Suchada could care less about the beautiful people, but her attention was caught by a chunky teenager with long hair and no make-up who scrambled behind the counter to act as salesgirl, asking the stars for their running-shoe sizes. It was the beginning of her twenty-year friendship with Nanthida, whom she would help to groom into a formidable businesswoman.

The money soon started rolling in for Nanthida, and she was looking for some way to use it. Her concert fee after the Hong Kong performance was 10,000 baht per hour—astoundingly high at the time. Her first business venture, in 1980, was Baan Nanthida, a 250-seat restaurant. Run by her sister Wichana, who loves to cook, Ban Nanthida proved a roaring success, and was helped by Nanthida's impromptu appearances to sing for the customers.

Nanthida's next investment plunge—a shoe store—was typical: she has Asia's biggest collection of shoes this side of Imelda Marcos. "That's because I was a singer," she explains. "I had to change stage outfits every day and find shoes to match. When I went out shopping, I was always buying shoes for the concerts."

So she switched to selling them. She opened her main shop—Next by Nanthida—in 1986, followed by four more branches in Bangkok and Chiang Mai.

"The whole idea started when I wanted to buy shoes for my niece. I was looking for real, high quality leather shoes—like the Italian brands I bought in Hong Kong—but I just couldn't find that quality in Bangkok. So I decided to make my own in my own shop.

"I contract the work out to several factories, for whatever aspect of shoe making each one does best. I consult with designers on what styles I like, and we try to decide what should be the newest fashion. My brother and sister help run the operation."

The tight-knit family forms "Kaewbuasai Incorporated." Occupying an honored role as family friend and advisor is Suchada Nimakorn. "Suchada is very close to my family," Nanthida says. "She's the one who always gives me advice. She even tells my dad what to do too. When she suggested that I enroll in an MBA course, I said, 'What? Every *day*?'A big problem for me." Nanthida rolls her eyes comically.

"But Suchada said no, you just go to class from four to seven each day, so you have time to perform at night. On Saturdays, the course ran from eight-thirty to four-thirty in the afternoon. Sometimes I had to go upcountry for concerts, but this was really a good chance for me to meet people who are experts in business. Some owned hotels and big companies and were very *kaeng* [talented]."

Nanthida graduated from Bangkok's prestigious Bordin Decha school, but always regretted her decision to quit her education when she became a professional singer. Suddenly, at age 28, she was at Thammasat University.

"I didn't know what I was doing there. I felt strange. I was ashamed when the teachers would ask, 'Do you know this?' And I would say, 'No. Zero!'" she wails and breaks into a peal of laughter.

Although accounting baffled her—"My sister still handles the books at the restaurant."—she found her courses in marketing and psychology extremely useful. "Things like the psychology of dealing with customers and employees—how to motivate them."

Nanthida employs a sales manager to supervise the salespeople in her shoe stores. She herself is on the phone every night to check how each store is doing, what styles are selling, and what not. Often, exhausted after a concert, she will visit a store to check stocks and receipts. But she still does not do her own accounts. "No, no, never. *Mai ow*! [No way]."

One benefit from her MBA course is a wide network of friends in the world of big business. "There were 57 of us on the course, and every three months we get together for a meal and some fun. I've made some really close friends, and any time I have a problem, I know the person to call."

Nanthida must be doing something right. Her forty million baht house, with its swimming pool and landscaped garden, is set in the exclusive Navatanee Estates. Amid the area's exquisite monuments to bad taste, her mansion is a graceful exception. Inside, the delicate harmony of her home furnishings is testimony to Nanthida's second grand passion: interior decoration. Her habit of constantly rearranging the furniture of her home has led to yet another business venture.

Her other shop—Nanthida's Knick & Knack & Nook—features the sort of curios, antiques, statuettes and paintings that she favors in her own home. "I love to decorate my home and to go out and shop for things, even if I don't buy them. It's fun. What I sell in this shop are things I want to buy myself. There's not enough room in my house, so I'm opening a shop!" she laughs. "And if no-one wants to buy something I like, I'll buy it myself. Even if it belongs to me, I'm gonna buy it."

The singer's schedule took her all over the world. She has performed in Los Angeles, Hong Kong, Singapore, Taiwan, Indonesia, Malaysia, the Philippines, London and Paris—picking up knick-knacks along the way.

"Singing's a lot better than being an actress, where you have to get up before dawn and work the whole day through. That's why I quit the movies. I prefer to concentrate on my singing. Before a concert, I'm really stressed out and nervous, but once the microphone is in my hand, I forget everything. When I'm out there entertaining an audience, I forget my body—who Nanthida is. Afterward, stress again."

"People ask me if I'll be lonely if I ever quit showbusiness, and I say no. I have my parents here, my friends. I love my home. It's where I spend my vacations. Most of the day I'm out meeting people. Why should I go out at night and meet more people? With all the demands on your time, you have to be in control."

When given the example of singer, Poompuang Duang-chand, who appears to have worked herself to death, Nan-thida nods vigorously. "It's a problem for most singers. They work so hard, even me. Sometimes you have no time to take care of yourself. But for me, my health is very important. My dad is concerned all the time. When I feel unwell, I go to the doctor right away. My vacations are also spent in the hospital."

She laughs at press rumors about her health. The same age as the late Poompuang, she was supposed to be suffering from the same ailments.

"People were handing me medicine—even a Bible—and recommending special doctors. You just have to keep yourself under control, even if people ask you the same question a hundred times a day. 'Are you really sick?' Even my secretary said, 'Don't lie to me. I won't tell anyone.' But you just say, 'No, I'm okay,' and you really feel *sabai jai* [happy] that everybody cares about you."

Summing up the philosophy of her hectic singer-cum-businesswoman life, Nanthida quotes fellow superstar, Thongchai "Bird" McIntyre. "He told me, 'We get really tired but we can't say we're bored.'"

Distracted by her pet dog, Rusty, who is busy trying to paw a hole in the tile floor, Nanthida says, "It helps to be crazy. I think some days that if you're *baa baa boh boh* [stark raving mad], it makes your life more beautiful. Even if you're trying to scratch a hole in the floor, you're happy. Make people *sabai jai*. Don't be serious all the time." She sighs, then perks up with another rich laugh. "So you can end this story by saying that Nanthida is a singing woman and a business-woman and she sounds like a crazy woman. *Baa baa boh boh!*"

The House that Eaton Built

The Tycoon—Raymond Eaton

The Moghul emperor Shah Jahan built the Taj Mahal as a monument to his marriage. Australian businessman Raymond Eaton built his thirty million baht house in Bangkok as a monument to his divorce.

After a seven-year marriage and a financially ruinous separation which left him homeless, Eaton decided to get on with his life and build a new house.

"The house is a personal statement," he says. "I wanted a new life and a fresh start. Thomas Wolfe wrote: 'A house is the social portrait of its owner.' Ultimately, the object is to use the house as a kind of salon where the good ambience will combine with good food, good wine and talk about art, literature, politics and sex. Anything but golf."

Eaton spent a year collecting his thoughts and studying the work of American architect Richard Meier. In terms of architecture, he wanted to combine four elements: form, color, texture and light. He approached Nithi Sthapitanonda, chairman of Architects 49 Ltd., and former president of the Association of Siamese Architects. Eight years earlier, Nithi had built Eaton's first house on Sukhumvit 39.

"We had a one-hour discussion," Eaton recalls. "I had a stack of plans. Khun Nithi is a strong person and he seemed uptight. He kept pushing me: 'Why do you want this? What do you want to do there?' OJ Simpson had an easier trial. Finally, after an hour, I said, 'You know, if you don't want to do this, I'll understand.' And he just broke out into a beatific smile: 'This is the house I've been dreaming of doing all my life. I just wanted to convince myself that you understand

that what you want is really radical. Don't get frightened halfway through. Don't panic.'"

Nithi recalls a sense of excitement for the project. "The style," he says, "is unique for Thailand, modern and simple, with a flat roof, exposed concrete, balanced geometrical forms—circles, squares, slanted lines—and a central courtyard with a pool that the house wraps itself around."

Nithi did all the drawings himself. Richard Meier was an influence, as was the Japanese architect Tadao Ando, but eventually he claims, "This was my own style, a totally new concept. Copies don't interest me. There's no creativity there. A client will bring me a photo and say, 'I want this.' So why waste your time with me? Why waste mine?"

With Eaton's house, Nithi did not even think about the time he was spending. "I'd go to the house while it was under construction and make minor changes. I was on the phone every day with Mr. Eaton. It's hard to find a client like him; one who gives you a chance to grow and do the best you can. The client and the architect are a team. We have to respect each other, depend on each other's good taste to select the best statements."

In this case, client and architect were in agreement about what they did not want. "My former house was L-shaped, with dining room and living room at each end—dead space," observes Eaton. "This house is designed for people. No part is isolated from other parts. Each flows into the next. The garden and house merge into each other, all rooms centered around the interior pool. My old house on Sukhumvit was stark, black and white. People called it 'the ice palace'."

Nithi feels the Sukhumvit house was dominated by Eaton's ex-wife's taste, whereas in the new house he took over all aspects: architecture, interior decoration and landscaping. "Mr. Eaton's selection of paintings, sculpture and furniture is special. There's nothing fancy about the house. You don't get lost in it. The house fits the person."

And exactly who is Raymond Eaton?

Born fifty years ago in Melbourne, he began working in retail sales right out of high school. While other young Australians headed for London's Kangaroo Valley in the early seventies, Eaton set his sights on Southeast Asia. He settled on Thailand in 1973, and after ten years with the PSA Group under Paul Sithi-Amnuay, he went into business for himself. In 1988, he was one of the first entrepreneurs to explore Vietnam's import-export market. Importing Thai office furniture to Vietnam, he exported garments and, later, gems and jewellry. As Integra Group president, he now has offices in Bangkok, Ho Chi Minh City, Hanoi and Hong Kong. Fluent in Thai, he has formed a wide range of friendships across Thailand's political, economic and cultural spectrum.

The house literally grew up around Eaton. After the external construction was completed in February 1995, he camped out in the empty shell and began the year-long task of interior decoration. "I wanted warmth and color," he says. "Art is an integral part of the house, not just decoration."

Every one of the house's 15 rooms is filled with paintings and sculptures. There are two Picassos and a Miro. Prominently displayed too are the established Thai artists Premik Suchaaritekul and Thaiwijit Pluangkasemsomboon. Eaton has known Thai artists for 23 years and, as a busienss pioneer in Vietnam, became a patron for impoverished painters there. "I prefer younger artists," he comments. "I've bought many works from students at Silapakorn. I find the younger artists not only cheaper but more creative."

Approached from the front, Eaton's house could be mistaken for an art gallery. The glass-walled entrance foyer is lined with sculptures on pedestals. A crowing rooster and a barking watchdog are made of scrap metal parts. Both were welded together by a police officer who moonlights as a sculptor.

A miniature waterfall and a 20-meter-long pool command the house's center space. Five shades of Italian glass give the pool a special clarity. To the left are the dining and kitchen areas. To the right is a glass turret that showcases the two Picassos. This leads to the living room and a media room, both facing the pool.

A spruce spiral staircase winds up the glass turret to a gallery dominated by a Gauguin-esque portrait of five nudes in a lush tropical setting. The gallery, which opens down to the living room below, is surrounded by an intricately-carved railing. Pointing out the workmanship, Eaton has high praise for his Thai construction crew. He notes that Robert Boughey, one of Thailand's top architects, has commented on the house's detailed craftsmanship in wood, metal, tile and glass.

"Bob Boughey asked me how I'd managed to achieve such quality," Eaton recalls. "I answered that I spent my weekends eating *somtam* with the crew. I was here all the time. My foreman commented that I was the first home owner who treated his crew like people."

Across the gallery are Eaton's quarters: master bedroom, walk-in closet, bathroom. His bed faces a glass wall and overlooks the swimming pool, the garden and the waterfall. The bedroom is a feature that Nithi is proud of, giving the house a sense of harmony.

"I like the long span of the master bedroom," Nithi comments. "It gives a feeling of control. I asked Mr. Eaton if he wanted glass walls and he said he could cope with it."

Beyond the bedroom is a book-lined study. There is a Buddhist altar, a Buddha photo by Tim Page, an ancient Burmese tapestry, and model cars. French windows open to a garden terrace. A glass frame over Eaton's desk displays a certificate testifying that he is an honorary Kentucky Colonel. "Just a reminder not to take this place too seriously," he says.

The house stands out in its Nichada Park neighborhood, a suburban development largely populated by expatriates and centered around the International School Bangkok campus off Chaeng Wattana Road.

"It's a refreshing break from the relentless Americana of the neighborhood," comments architect Boughey. "And it's beautiful at night."

Summing up his feelings about the house, Nithi says, "I love it. I'm proud of it. It's one of my best."

Eaton recently took a step toward establishing the multicultural salon of his dreams when his home served as the site of a party hosted by *New Yorker* magazine for its advertisers and suppliers. The previous party was held at a 17th-century Lisbon castle. The theme of this party was "Uncovering the New Face of Bangkok". The 100-odd guests were treated to Bangkok's finest music, poetry, art, fashion and food.

A translucent shield was placed over the pool, making it a catwalk for a Thai fashion show. A folk chorus sang and danced to traditional music. Poet Angkan Galayanapong recited his work in Thai chanting style. Painter Thesiri Suksopha created canvasses accompanied by music. Supermodel Rojana (Yui) Phetkanha compered the fashion show.

Summing up his life, Raymond Eaton suggests his own tombstone epitaph: "Made millions, lost millions, had a good time."

Romancing the Rails

The Railroad Workers

Leaving daily from Bangkok to Sungai Golok at the Malaysian border, the State Railway of Thailand (SRT) Rapid Train #45 is the slow train. It is also the poor man's train; only two of its 28 passenger cars are sleepers. A third-class seat for the 1,159km trip costs 210 baht. For this price, you sit up for 22 hours on a thinly-padded bench. Sleep becomes a gymnastic feat. For 384 baht more, you can stretch out in the luxury of your own curtained bunk. But, for a lot of people, 384 baht is a lot of money—over two days' work at the minimum wage.

Photographer Jonathan Taylor is not satisfied with his second-class sleeper.

"Why didn't you book an air-conditioned car?" he wants to know.

"Because the windows fog up and you can't take pictures," I reply confidently.

"You can't take pictures from a moving train anyway."

"O."

"Maybe we can upgrade our tickets."

"There's no air-conditioned car on this train."

"O."

And our window is stuck shut. A friendly conductor bashes at the frame with a wooden wedge, then ferrets about with a screwdriver. No luck. We are resigned to 1,159 very hot kilometers.

The train pulls out of Hualamphong Station at precisely 1:30 p.m. An hour later, we are out of Bangkok and into the smells of mud and dung: rice paddies, bamboo groves, fish farms, vegetable plots, sugar cane plantations.

We are traveling on the line that was laid out by British engineer, H. Gittins, who, after working on the Canadian transcontinental line, came to Thailand in 1888 to survey lines to Chiang Mai and Nakhon Ratchasima.

In 1909, as chief engineer of the Southern Railway, he began laying track from Petchaburi, reaching Songkhla in 1915, and the Malaysian border three years later. The workers were mainly Chinese immigrants, and, as they hacked their way through primal jungle, a good number were carried off by tigers.

In the restaurant car, we introduce ourselves to a railway policeman, who leads us forward to the crew car to meet the head conductor. We pass through three compartments of reclining seats, occupied partly by European backpackers whose bare feet are crossed at the ankles and propped up atop the headrests in front of them. We cringe.

The third-class carriages are asprawl with bodies desperately contorted for comfort: amorous teenagers entangled in blue jeans, squalling babies, incompetent mothers, Muslim elders in skullcaps, women in black cowls, saffron-robed monks, turbaned Sikhs, and Chinese matrons in pajama suits.

People read comic books, bob their heads to Walkman earphones, scoop up curry-and-rice, crack peanuts, slice fruit, sip on beer cans through straws, smoke cigarettes, and nod off to sleep. Heads flop in all directions. The railway cop tells a teenager to turn down his ghetto-blaster.

Trim, gray-haired, dignified, head conductor Chanat Mapinit welcomes us to the crew car. At his desk piled with invoices and schedules, he tells us proudly that he began working for the railroad in 1957. His salary has since risen from 540 baht to 10,900 baht a month. His colleague, Sompet Surian, joins us from the neighboring bunkroom, where he has been taking a nap. They will rotate duty when they reach Surat Thani, halfway down the coast. Both have traveled on every route on Thailand's 3,780km of track, and both are due to retire next year when they reach sixty.

Sompet shows us through the freight car, piled with boxed television and stereo sets, rice cookers, newspapers and motorcycles. "Everything in here," he comments, before leading us forward to the bunkroom he shares with Chanat. Another bunkroom houses the engine driver team. Train crews work two 2,318km round trips on; one off.

Further forward are a half dozen third-class benches and a couple of hammocks where the junior staff sleep: three conductors, two brakemen, and three railway policemen. Casually dressed in T-shirts and sarongs, they lounge about, joking and laughing, until Jonathan enters with his camera— which prompts them to quickly doff hammocks and don uniforms. "Right!" Jonathan laughs. "Just the picture I didn't want."

By the time we work our way back through third-class to the restaurant car, all the kids and half the adults are asleep. The foresighted have brought mats upon which they curl up on the floor. Others make do with spread newspapers.

In the restaurant car, teenage waiters offer various reasons for working on the railroad. Waiter Burai Boonshuan from Khon Kaen is typical. "I was out of school and this was a job. It got me out of Khon Kaen."

The restaurant staff work for a private contractor—with no fixed salary, but a share in the profits. Burai's share averages 2,500 baht a month. "I like the travel," he adds. "The only problem is when we want to close the restaurant car and people are drunk and don't want to leave. That's when we call the police. It happens once or twice a month."

We reach the postcard-pretty railway station at Hua Hin at 6 p.m. Resort towers, visible on the horizon, line the shore. They are the only high-rises between Bangkok and Hat Yai. An hour later, we are plunging through darkness, the landscape illuminated only by neon-lit prawn ponds, aeration paddles ceaselessly turning. At Prachuab Khiri Khan, when we navigate our way back to our sleeping berths, we find that third-class has emptied slightly, allowing some passengers the luxury of stretching out on the four-foot benches. Four feet might not sound like much, but it is quite adequate if you are five feet worth of Thai.

Sleeping car attendant, Sunthorn Charleonphan, a twenty-year railroad veteran, has already made up our bunks. Born on a farm in Ayuthaya, he had dreamed as a schoolboy of working on the railroad. "I like my job," he says. "Except maybe the money's not enough. But then, with a wife and kids, money is never enough."

We awake at 6 a.m. to the sound of Sunthorn slamming bunks back into seats; to vendors' cries of "cafe lon" (*hot coffee*); and to the brilliant green of Thailand's Deep South: emerald paddy fields and endless rows of rubber trees. Here, you see mosques rather than *wats*; goats rather than pigs; men in sarongs; women in ankle-length gowns; schoolgirls in identical black cowls. At Yala station, Sunthorn helps us off with our luggage and we are suddenly surrounded by fierce faces—dark-skinned, big-eyed, wavy-haired, toothy-grinned, hatchet-nosed—the classic Southern Thai amalgam of Indian, Arab, Bugis and Malay blood. Everyone speaks *Yawi*, the Malay dialect of the border provinces.

○ ○ ○

A few days later, we are in Hat Yai—a Chinese city of sharks-fin and birds-nest restaurants, high-rise luxury hotels, and low-rent massage parlors—ready to board a train back to Bangkok.

Hat Yai was founded by the railroad at the junction where two lines fork down to the border towns of Sungai Golok and Padang Besar (a branch line to Songkhla was closed in 1977). A photograph of Hat Yai in 1924 depicts a tropical

Dodge City, with shop signs in Chinese. As ex-railroad laborers turned to rubber growing and tin mining, Hat Yai boomed to become the economic capital of the South. The fastest-growing city in Thailand, Hat Yai remains a major hub for the national railroad network, which carries 71 million passengers and eight million tons of freight every year.

Our train is late. Scheduled to arrive from Sungai Golok at 3:55 p.m., Rapid Train #46 wheezes into the station at 6:30. In the sleeping car, we meet Sunthorn again. He greets us with a grin and a *wai,* and tells us that the delay on the line was caused by a collision the day before up in Thonburi. Two men in a pickup truck were killed trying to race across a railroad intersection. A substitute locomotive had to be found and dispatched down south.

Our fellow passengers are mostly dressed in full Muslim regalia. Bearded men wear white *haji* robes and turbans; women, richly-embroidered gowns or full black *chalor*. Sunthorn explains that they are attending a Muslim conference in Pattaya.

Pattaya?

In the restaurant car, Jonathan orders up a shrimp salad, but fails to finish more than a mouthful. The trick in ordering railway food is to keep it simple: fried rice, sausages, omelets. Anything more complicated is inviting disaster.

At breakfast the next morning, we meet one of the three cooks. Sleepy-eyed Nat Nangsuthem, 26, is from Pattani, where her parents own a rubber farm. She tells us she has been working on the railway for seven months, averaging an income of 3,500 baht.

Where did she learn how to cook?

"At home," she shrugs. "All Thai women know how to cook."

"Do you have any problems with this kind of work?"

"Only that I'm tired all the time. It's hard to sleep on the train."

A sudden commotion erupts in the restaurant car. Waiters are whooping and shouting with excitement.

The news?

There has been another railway collision: a ten-wheel truck in Nakhon Pathom. The train backs up past a road junction in Nong Praduk, and we settle down for a long hot wait. A crowd of Muslims and backpackers abandon the train and mill around a bus stop. At 11:10 a.m., after a delay of two hours and forty minutes, the train lurches forward again. At 12:50, we finally cross the Chao Praya into Bangkok. "I never thought I'd be so pleased to see Bangkok," Jonathan says.

We arrive at Hualamphong Station at 1:30 p.m.—five hours late—and immediately buy tickets for the next morning's 6:15 a.m. train to Nong Khai, 625km north. There are eighty people ahead of us in the queue, but thanks to the computerized booking system, we have tickets in hand in only a half hour.

○ ○ ○

At 5:30 a.m. the next morning, Hualamphong is surprisingly abustle. Shops are open and hundreds of passengers sit, or squat, amid their luggage. Out on platform #5, two train drivers are sharing a smoke beside the big GE diesel locomotive. Narin Charoenphan is the senior driver, making a monthly salary of 20,500 baht. His father was a train engineer too, and he has been driving trains since he graduated from the SRT locomotive school thirty years ago. Turkiet Kieputna is his assistant. Twelve years on the job, he earns 10,100 baht a month. The two drivers swap four-hour shifts.

Narin points to a neighboring platform and a brand-new GE diesel locomotive. "I don't know how to drive that one yet," he says with a grin. The GE diesel is one of 25—together with twenty Daewoo models—recently ordered by the SRT to boost its total locomotive fleet to 527.

Our fellow passengers this morning are a young lot, many of them students returning home from final exams in Bangkok schools. There is a festive air and a few guitars are being passed around. The Northeastern faces are strikingly different from the Southern Thai: finer boned and lighter skinned, with snub noses rather than hatchets. There are no backpackers.

This is another poor man's train: 17 third-class cars (153 baht) and a single wooden car with dusty reclining seats (268 baht). Sharing the reclining seats with us are a Thai-Chinese businessman visiting a friend in Udon Thani, a monk returning to his *wat* in Nong Khai, and a soldier on home leave to Khon Kaen. In front of us are two sisters from Nong Khai—Daeng and Bo—and Daeng's two little slaphappy kids who keep us entertained for hours.

By 7:30, we are out of Bangkok and passing through the brightly-painted farmhouses and rich paddy fields of the central flood plain. Straw-hatted farmers push roto-tillers and ride all-purpose *e-tans*. But two hours later, as the train chugs off the flood plain up toward the Korat plateau, the countryside empties out into dusty scrub studded with a few forlorn trees. When these railway tracks were laid, sixty years ago, this area was virgin forest.

The landscape now is barren. Low hills bake in a heat haze; thin cattle graze on rice stubble; a few dried-up plots of corn and cotton are scattered amid burnt-over badlands. The hills rise higher into scabrous cones, and the track runs along a 100-foot embankment providing a miles-wide view of a yellow valley floor dotted with a few puffs of green. There is not a house in sight.

We pass though sheer rock cuttings in rolling hill country, mile after mile of desolation interrupted by cassava and eucalyptus plots. You can feel the heat coming off the ground.

The wind rushes in the window like a blast furnace. Three hours of this has a soporific effect. All our neighbors have nodded off.

Just after midday, we reach the halfway point: Bua Yai in Northern Nakhon Ratchasima. Jonathan joins the drivers up in the locomotive. The land stretches flat as a pancake now until we reach the first oasis in the desert. Khon Kaen is bustling with factories, warehouses and tractor dealerships. There is even a seedy golf course. At 4 p.m. we stop at Udon Thani and the countryside finally turns greener with sugar cane plantations. The train pulls into tiny Nong Khai station—precisely on time—fifty minutes later.

○ ○ ○

The next night, we give ourselves a break: the air-conditioned 7 p.m. express to Bangkok. We meet up with the station master, Wisit Prungpat, who tells us he has been working for the railroad for 29 years, rising through the ranks to his current post at a salary of 26,140 baht. "Before the railroad, I was a monk for nine years," he says. "After I left the monkhood, I needed money, and I love trains. With the new Friendship Bridge in Nong Khai, our passenger volume is rising. I handle 11 trains a day. And there's a bigger demand for sleeping cars. There's more money here now."

The night express has 22 cars: one first-class with private compartments; two air-con sleepers; five with fans; one with reclining seats; and 13 third-class cars. As soon as we settle in, we are set upon by two pretty long-haired waitresses who—with identical dimpled smiles—are very determined to sell us beer. "We work on commission," explains Sin Kasburum, elegant in a brass-buttoned blue blazer. "You sell a lot, you get a lot."

Sin and her sister-in-law, Vandee, allow us to buy them Cokes instead. They are from a poor village in Sisaket called

Ban Yang, where their five-*rai* plot of land does not provide enough rice to live on. "The land is very poor and dry," Vandee says. "It's a hard life. No work, no money."

"I've been doing this job for five years," Sin says. "I like working on the train. I have a lot of friends up and down the line. We work 15 round trips a month, with a week off home."

Vandee is married to Sin's older brother, Lek, a ten-year railroad veteran, who is supervisor of the restaurant car. While they are on the train, Lek's parents take care of their 11-year-old son and Sin's two teenage daughters. Another sister, Pen Kasburum, 18 and still single, works on the same train. Off duty, the four rolling Kasburums all share the same house in Ban Yang. "I make maybe 3,000 baht a month and I send half home for my kids," Vandee says. "I'd like to be with them all the time, but I have to work."

Next morning, we arrive in Bangkok after 62 hours and 3,300km on a locomotive yo-yo. At 6:15 a.m.—five minutes early—the Nong Khai train pulls into Hualamphong Station. It is just one of 26 to arrive this morning from all parts of Thailand. Passengers sling bags and babies over their shoulders; pass down baskets and bundles to pushcart porters; and march silently along the gloom of the platform. Emerging into Bangkok's first light, they hail taxis and *tuk-tuks*, and scatter into the maw of the city.

On the Road Again

The Truckers

Abdul Musalate and Abdullah Tamate leave Pattani on a Sunday morning for the 1,050km haul to Bangkok aboard a two-trailer Isuzu truck. Twenty-one hours later—a fast run—they pull into the office of the Pattani Saha Southern Trailer Transport Company, a dusty bare-concrete shophouse on Riap Maenam Road in Bangkok's port district. They sleep that night in the cab of the truck, make deliveries of rubber and para wood the next day, and on Wednesday are ready for the long haul back down to Pattani.

At noon, their ten-wheel truck is loaded with sacks of prawn feed, but their second trailer is only half full with a grab-bag cargo of steel pipes, knock-down office furniture, floor tiles, stationery, pump motors and drums of glue. Abdul and Abdullah sit on sacks of fertilizer reading Thai comic books and trading quips in *Yawi*, the Malay dialect of their native Pattani. Dispatcher Yusof Maming is busy on the phones. "It's a slow day today," he observes. "Yesterday, our trucks were full and out of here."

Yusof is also from Pattani, a childhood friend and school-mate of Pattani Saha owner, Prasit Tapawahsin. "Almost all our drivers are Pattani Muslims," Yusof notes. "They're dependable and they don't drink. And only very rarely do they take *yaa baa* [amphetamine pills]."

At 2:45 p.m., a pickup delivers bales of paper, plastic sheeting and ping-pong balls. An hour later, another load arrives: aluminum stepladders, steel bolts, shackles and chains. Four teenage loaders top off the cargo with plastic chicken feeders, waterers, egg cartons and transport cages—everything a chicken needs from egg to slaughterhouse.

Abdul and Abdullah secure the load with chains and turnbuckles, and tie a tarpaulin down tight over the tall wood-slat sides of the truck. Abdul backs-up the ten-wheeler to the extra trailer; Abdullah couples the two together and plugs in the electric cables that will power the rear trailer's brake and tail lights. A quick sluice bath in the back of the shophouse and they are ready to go. It is just after 5 p.m.

Abdul climbs behind the wheel, I take the passenger seat, and Abdullah stretches out on a cushion over the engine between us. Compared to American rigs, the Isuzu cab is Spartan. There is no CB radio—no radio of any kind—and the air conditioner does not work. There is only a narrow sleeping shelf behind the seats. The engine has a modest five gears. "Volvos and Benzes have ten and 14," Abdul informs me.

As we ascend the approach to the Rama IX Bridge, a spectacular panorama of Bangkok and the Chao Praya spreads out below us. "I've got four teenage kids in Pattani," Abdul says. "I wouldn't want to raise them in Bangkok. But I took this job—for 7,000 baht a month—so my kids would have a chance to go to university. I average a week home a month."

We inch up the bridge's steep incline in first gear. Abdul predicts that this is going to be a tough trip. Heavy rainstorms have been swamping the South for the past six weeks: flash floods, mud slides, washed out bridges. Twenty schools in Yala have just closed down because of the floods.

"This trip is going to take 24 hours for sure," Abdul says with a grim smile. He knows the route well, having driven up and down it for 15 years. At 51, he has enough squint wrinkles to make Clint Eastwood look baby-faced.

We roll down the southern end of the bridge and onto the expressway to Samut Sakhon. Abdullah crawls in the back to sleep. We have been on the road for an hour now, and the sun is a giant red ball hanging over miles of dense traffic. By sundown, we reach Samut Sakhon—a flat industrial wasteland of factories, canneries, and reeking fish mills.

At Petchaburi, we turn off to Highway 4. Pickups full of female chicken pluckers pass us on the road. Abdullah wakes up and sniffs the foul night air. "Lots of busy chickens out there," he comments.

At 8:30, we stop for dinner at a truckstop in Cha-am. The restaurant is Muslim and the waitresses speak *Yawi*. The drink cooler is scrupulously devoid of beer, but chock full of liquid speed: Total, Lipo and Kratin Daeng. A table of four company drivers wait for us. Their two trucks will accompany us in a convoy to Pattani. Other drivers are on their way up to Bangkok. They pose happily for photos. One driver asks me, "Do you want some medicine to keep you awake?"

"*Yaa baa*?"

"I'm on it right now. But only because I'm driving alone. There's no other way to stay up all night."

Dinner proves that cuisine is not one of the glories of Islam: *Beef Gristle Soup, Beef and Horrible Green Vegetable, Ancient Beef and Greasy Onions*. . . .The drivers order coffee and smoke cigarettes, joking around in *Yawi* until Abdul, the convoy leader, says, "*Pergi*" ["Let's go"].

A half hour later, we are on the coastal road leading into Hua Hin.

"Ten years ago, there was nothing here," Abdul remarks, gesturing at the ranks of luxury hotels lighting up the night sky. "I've seen a lot of changes on this road. We used to worry about bandits at night. Not anymore."

By midnight, we are in Prachuab Khiri Khan, 130km north of Chumphon. The night belongs to the trucks now. Making up 90% of the traffic, they are a constant procession of blue, green and red lights.

We stop for gas and coffee at a truckstop, and find the other drivers in a state of grinning excitement. They report that fifty meters from the Muslim restaurant in Cha-am, a

Mitsubishi Lancer came speeding out of a feeder road and crashed broadside into the rear trailer of a Bangkok-bound company truck. The car driver and his passenger were unconscious with bleeding head wounds. "You missed a great picture!" one trucker tells me.

Over coffee and cigarettes, the drivers shrug off the chances of accidents, saying that they look forward to driving someday to China and Vietnam. The night has turned cold, and the drivers are bundled up in sweaters, denim jackets and towel turbans. We take off for Chumphon a half hour later with Abdullah at the wheel now. He has swigged a half bottle of Lipo, but depends mainly on cigarettes to keep alert. "At home, I barely smoke a pack in two days. On the road, it's a pack and a half per trip."

I fall asleep at 4 a.m. and wake up at 6:30—70km north of Surat Thani—to a sodden green landscape of flooded rice fields. Ground mist is rising with the dawn. We pass plantations of rubber, coconut, oil palm and coffee, and stands of bamboo, banana, mango, pepper and cashew nut.

At 7:30 a.m., we bypass Surat Thani and head straight south for Thung Song, 133km through the heart of flood country: swollen, brown rivers, uprooted trees, sunken rubber plantations. Two hours later, we stop for a conference with a Bangkok-bound company trucker who warns of major floods in Phattalung, 100km south.

At 11 a.m., in a steady drizzle, we stop in Thung Song for gas and a quick lunch of omelet and coffee. Abdul changes a tire that he thinks looks ready for a blow-out, and takes the wheel again. We pass a third police checkpoint. So far, we have not been stopped or weighed.

"I've never been arrested or had to pay a fine," Abdul says. "Getting weighed is just a matter of luck. Sometimes twice a month, other times you'll go two or three months without getting pulled over. If you're stopped, you have to know how to talk to the police. It's better to pay 100 baht than risk a 2,000 baht fine and jail. The owners always give us a couple of hundred baht in case of trouble."

The rain suddenly turns heavy. Heading into Phattalung, the sides of the road are raging streams, 20–40 feet wide. Roadside houses are islands in brown ponds. The road is slippery and Abdul slows down from his steady 60kph. The intersection to Phattalung is two feet under water. We navigate for a couple of kilometers, forging between pickups and motorcycles, until we reach dry road again. We have another 150km to go before Hat Yai. The road undulates over hilly terrain, we slow to a crawl on the inclines, and the rain falls more heavily than ever.

At 3:30 p.m., the convoy reaches the ring road around Hat Yai, heads down the new highway to Chana, and along the gulf coast for the last 100km to Pattani. The rain never stops, but the road is straight and flat, and we reach the Pattani Saha office at 5:20 p.m.—just a little over 24 hours after leaving Bangkok, as Abdul had predicted.

The drivers turn in their bills of lading to the dispatcher and are free to go home. Tomorrow, they will make deliveries throughout Pattani province and into neighboring Yala and Narathiwat, and then Abdul and his friends can look forward to two whole days off. On Monday, they will head back to Bangkok.

Conversion of the Body Snatchers

The Emergency Medical Crews

Ewen Campbell, the production editor, closed the next day's edition of his newspaper and stopped for a beer at the Joy Luck Club, a journalists' hangout on Banglamphu's Phra Athit Road.

An hour later, he stepped across the street to flag a taxi home. He was standing before the old riverside fort at the curve in the road when two teenagers lost control of their speeding motorcycle, ran him over, and smashed into the wall of the fort. One of the youths died instantly; the other a few minutes later. Both had massive head injuries. Neither were wearing helmets. Ewen Campbell was sprawled in agony, his right kneecap shattered.

Friends rushed out of the bar and frantically punched numbers on their mobile phones to summon an ambulance. That was when they learned that the city's most prominent hospitals do not have emergency ambulance services.

What Bangkok does have are the "body snatchers"—the Ruamkatanyu and Por Tek Tueng foundations, whose young volunteers make merit by retrieving corpses from the city streets.

Within five minutes, Ruamkatanyu volunteers in their jumpsuit uniforms arrived at the accident scene to bundle the two bodies into their pickup truck. Ewen's friends crouched at his side, holding his hand as agonizing minutes ticked by. His face was white with pain.

Every year, thousands of people with broken bones and internal injuries are simply hoisted into passing taxis, *tuk-*

tuks and Ruamkatanyu pickup trucks. Many might have survived if it were not for the clumsy attention they received at the roadside.

Ewen was luckier. After 15 minutes, an ambulance with red lights flashing and siren blaring, sped down Phra Athit Road. Out jumped Dr. Wimol Siriwasin, and together with a nurse and a medical technician, she soon had the victim stabilized in the ambulance.

"Because he's a *farang*, we'll take him to Bangkok Nursing Home," Dr. Wimol said. As the ambulance sped off, she radioed ahead details of the patient's injury and his pulse and blood pressure to the emergency room of the hospital. Ewen was in safe hands.

Dr. Wimol and her team are members of the Narenthorn Emergency Medical Service (EMS), based at Rajavithi Hospital. This free ambulance service is one of only two in Bangkok. The second is at Wachira Hospital.

"The need is obvious," says Dr. Tairjing Sirihanich, director of the Narenthorn EMS. "A lot of people arrive at emergency rooms when it's too late to help them. They die alone, bleeding to death in a *tuk-tuk*, because there's no-one around to apply a tourniquet. Others die of shock, bumped around in traffic. Many lives can be saved within the first 15 minutes with emergency medical care."

According to health ministry statistics, two people die every hour in traffic accidents in Thailand. For people aged 15–40, traffic injuries are the number one cause of death. Economic losses are nine billion baht annually.

"In Bangkok, we've long had emergency fire services," notes Dr. Tairjing. "It's time we had an emergency medical service as well."

The Narenthorn EMS has six ambulances stationed at Rajavithi, and another two each at branch hospitals in Noparat and Lard Sin. The most modern are equipped with defibrillators, respirators, oxygen tanks, cervical collars, splints, endotracheal tubes, IV sets, surgical gear, and emergency medicines such as adrenaline, glucose, morphine, pethidine and xylocaine.

"The problem isn't that there aren't enough ambulances, but quality, trained personnel," says Dr. Tairjing. "For manpower—ambulance drivers and EMS technicians—we depend on the Por Tek Tueng and Ruamkatanyu volunteers, who like to do this kind of job. Funding comes from Rajavithi Hospital, the two voluntary foundations, and the World Health Organization. Our stress now is quality training before quantity. This is a pilot project. Hopefully, once we solve problems and pinpoint the most important needs, the government can follow up."

Initial "front-line" training for volunteers—18 hours at weekends at Rajavithi—is provided by Dr. Somchai Kanchanasut, director of the hospital's Emergency Medical Department.

Working off the Internet, Dr. Somchai has translated into Thai the standard, eight-volume American text on basic emergency care. "So far we've trained 200 volunteers, who are the first responders to an emergency," Dr. Somchai notes. "Eventually we hope to train up to 1,000."

The primary course covers such topics as basic life signals, air ways, cardiovascular emergencies, diabetes shock, altered mental states, obstetrics, skeletal and soft tissue injuries, head and spine injuries, drug overdoses, burns, blood loss and shock. Technicians learn wound dressing and bandaging; the use of tourniquets and splints; and cardiopulmonary resuscitation. Eventually they will master the two-man, multi-step procedure for removing the motorcycle helmet from a rider suspected of cervical injury.

This is an operation sorely needed in Bangkok. Of the 1,322 emergency patients cared for in Narenthorn EMS's first year of service, 78% were victims of traffic accidents. Two-thirds of these were motorcycle riders—overwhelmingly young and male. Peak period for injuries are the drinking hours between 11 p.m. and 2 a.m.

Dr. Wimol recalls a case where a young motorcycle accident victim was alert and talking to his rescuers, but when they lifted him into their pickup truck, he died instantly of cervical injury. Rule one of emergency medical care is, "Above all, do no harm."

A gynecological surgeon, and head of the Sexually Transmitted Disease Department, Dr. Wimol is one of ten Rajavithi doctors who staff the Narenthorn center, along with 16 registered nurses, who have received an eighty-hour training course from an Australian ambulance team.

The Narenthorn center is a two-story building that earlier served as Rajavithi's emergency room. The first floor houses a communications center where attendants monitor a bank of radios that alert the center to police and foundation emergency calls. Upstairs is the crew lounge. There is a bunkroom for the drivers and technicians, separate quarters for doctors and nurses, a long table for communal meals, and a TV and VCR.

Above the TV is a framed painting of *Phra* Tai Tong Koom, a wandering Chinese monk of the Sung dynasty, who is the spiritual founder of the Por Tek Tueng Foundation. During a flooding of the Yangtze, the monk retrieved corpses from the river to prevent a cholera plague. The cult, which grew up around *Phra* Tai Tong Koom, was brought to Bangkok by Chinese immigrants and became the Por Tek Tueng Foundation in 1909.

With a similar corpse-collecting mandate, Ruamkatanyu followed in 1970. The two foundations take alternate patrols in Bangkok's streets, north and south of Petchaburi Road—a "green line" established in 1992 after a series of brawls over who had rights to what corpse.

On duty one night were Ruamkatanyu volunteers, Narongpong Tantakul and Boonkiet Wicharot. Ambulance driver Narongpong, 29, has been with Ruamkatanyu for ten years, and with Narenthorn since its foundation. A Ramkamhaeng student, he also helps out at his father's slaughterhouse in Yannawa. His hobbies are target shooting and racing a souped-up Toyota. Technician Boonkiet, a native of Banglamphu, was on duty the night of Ewen Campbell's accident.

"I know that corner well," he says. "Kids race motorcycles down the straight of Phra Athit and then come to the curve. That's where garbage trucks load and the road is greasy. A lot of kids die there."

A buzzer sounds and the crew—Narongpong, Boonkiet, Dr. Wimol, and nurse Kanchana Muangsakorn—scramble for the ambulance. Flipping on siren and flashers, Narongpong whips the ambulance into heavy traffic around the Victory Monument. Boonkiet juggles a loudspeaker microphone and a walkie-talkie, warning motorists to pull aside while getting directions to the accident site. The victims are two motorcyclists in Hway Kwang, one seriously injured.

The ambulance screams up the expressway ramp, tops 130kph as it weaves through lanes, and then descends upon the traffic-packed mayhem of Rachadapisek Road.

"Please move left, please move left!" calls Boonkiet. "Thank you, thank you!"

Time speeds up like in a demented arcade game as Narongpong—never touching the brake—accelerates through holes in traffic, narrowly misses a motorcycle and a red sports car, and spins into a G-force U-turn across four lanes of oncoming vehicles. Finally, on a darkened side street, the ambulance screeches to a halt at a gathering of police cars and foundation pickups.

At a four-way intersection, two teenagers on a motorcycle have collided with a pickup truck. One kid is limping with minor abrasions on his leg; the other is supine on the pavement. He is conscious, if somewhat groggy.

Pulling on rubber gloves, Dr. Wimol asks questions, probes his leg, and checks his pupils for signs of brain damage. The victim is Rachan Kumka, 22, a factory worker. Dr. Wimol suspects a fractured pelvis. Once he is transferred into the ambulance, she records his vital signs. Narongpong guns the ambulance back to the emergency room.

No sooner is the crew back than they are off again—but at a more sedate speed. The victim is nearby, and only slightly injured. The motorcyclist, ironically enough, is a policeman from the 191 Emergency Rescue Unit. After enjoying some off-duty beers, he had misjudged the timing of a red light.

Back in the crew lounge again, Narongpong recalls a wide variety of emergency runs: falls, burns, electrical shocks, heart attacks, child births, suicide attempts, factory accidents, knife and gunshot wounds.

According to Narenthorn statistics, average ambulance response time is ten minutes. Distance and traffic naturally factor into this equation. For particularly horrendous traffic jams, police at Phaya Thai and other stations provide motorcycle escorts.

As the night grows later, other Ruamkatanyu volunteers in their multi-zippered-and-patched *Top Gun* jumpsuits, drift through the lounge. While single men in their twenties predominate among the crew members, perhaps one in ten are women.

Natagan Lamool, twenty, works as a sales clerk at the Robinson Department Store on the opposite side of the Victory Monument to Rajavithi Hospital.

Why did she join Ruamkatanyu?

"I like to help society," she answers simply.

Sumali "Bee" Puksatawepho, a senior at Kasetsart University majoring in public health, has a slightly different answer. "This kind of work is *sanuk* [fun]. Otherwise, I'd just waste time on a *tiao* [excursion]."

The men in her crew are Samak Sipayak, a sophomore at Don Muang Technical College, and Banlursak Laochan, a senior law student at Bangkok University.

"Many of the volunteers are quite well-educated," comments Dr. Wimol. "This makes the training courses much easier."

The uniform, the camaraderie, the adrenaline thrill of the chase—all contribute to increase the volunteer rolls. But the essence of volunteerism is religious—to make merit through the performance of good deeds. Public perception of the "body snatchers," however, is tainted by allegations of theft.

Boonkiet contends that volunteers of the big Ruamkatanyu and Por Tek Tueng foundations enlist for religious and moral reasons, but there are a half dozen small foundations, plus freelance body snatchers, whose motives are not so lofty.

"I can only talk about Ruamkatanyu," he says. "A couple of weeks ago, an accident victim accused us of stealing his gold chain. Narongpong was very angry at the charge. We take people's property very seriously. We cooperate with the police—who are responsible for inventories and notifying relatives—and we swear an oath not to steal, and to work as a united team for the sake of making merit. In the case of the gold necklace, the patient later remembered that he gave it to the hospital's X-ray technician, who passed it on to a relative."

But he does recall another case in which the Ruamkatanyu volunteer was guilty. "He stole a man's expensive belt and was reported by other volunteers. He was taken before the abbot, Luang Poh Biem. When he denied the charges, the abbot said he would be cursed if he was lying. Immediately afterwards, he was run over by a car. He lasted two days in the ICU, then he died."

The buzzer sounds again and the ambulance crew races off to a deserted stretch of Kampheng Phet II Road along the railroad tracks. Two motorcyclists are sprawled alongside the road. Police on the scene have a weird tale to tell. Somehow, a boulder was deposited mysteriously on this dark section of road.

Did it fall off the back of a truck?

Whatever the reason, Somsak Komdej, 27, slammed into the boulder, which ripped off his front tire and sent him flying over the handlebars. Right behind him, a couple crashed their bike into his. Chaira Monkuk was uninjured; Surapong Rangsup suffered a dozen deep facial cuts. Somsak is quickly stabilized with suspected cervical injuries. All were wearing helmets, which probably saved their lives.

Back at Rajavithi, the crew drifts off to bed. The last one up is Sumitra Beyanakoon, a newly-graduated doctor from Rangsit University. She recalls the hectic time at the New Year's holiday: traffic accidents, drunken fights and cardiopulmonary cases.

"I've probably seen three cases a month where the patient would have died without prompt treatment," she says. "This is satisfying work."

The Road to Hell Is Not Paved

The Journalist (Reporter's Notebook 4)

I am a connoisseur of bad roads: Sierra Leone's Kabala Track, Brazil's TransAmazonic Highway, the infamous Phnom Penh–Battambang "Dancing Road," and, in general, Laos. In Kanchanaburi, I found the very worst: 171km of hideous jungle track, a fit venue for a test drive of Chrysler's Jeep Cherokee.

The Chrysler management team drove a convoy of 11 Cherokees from Bangkok to Kanchanaburi. Here, a dozen journalists—after a briefing on the Jeep's four-wheel-drive transmission—were allowed to bash around the hillocks and bogs of the KC Motocross Circuit. Owner Taksin Boonpongsa would lead us the next day on a ten-hour test drive through the jungle.

I was not prepared for the sheer power of the Jeep Cherokee's 4 liter, 190 horsepower engine. The only off-road vehicle I had driven before was a Land Rover, back in 1971 in Africa. While built like a tank, the old Land Rover was slow and cumbersome, with a bone-rattling suspension. The Jeep Cherokee fairly flew through the motocross obstacle course—up and down steep earth ramps, around muddy curves, through bogs and ponds—while, behind the wheel, I floated on a cushiony multi-leaf suspension system, enjoying all the extras the old Land Rover lacked: comfortable seat, power steering, power brakes, and air conditioning.

Making two circuits of the track, I hadn't had so much fun since I was a kid crashing bumper cars at Coney Island—with the added thrill that, in my hands, I had a 1.3 million baht state-of-the-art vehicle to wreck.

On my second lap, with Taksin in the shotgun seat, I stomped the pedal to the metal and shot over the steepest ramp—the windshield filled with nothing but sky—flew over a second crest, and careened down toward a narrow log bridge. "Easy! Easy!" Taksin howled. "You have plenty of power. You don't need to push it." When Taksin took the wheel, he negotiated the course with smooth, elegant finesse.

Next morning, I slid behind the wheel again for the big, real-life jungle course, feeling like Jackie Stewart. Never mind that I had not driven a car in five years, since my wife sold our pickup truck, which she would not let me drive anyway, after I crashed it into a cow (cow's fault).

My colleagues were Sombat Meethaikae and Weeravuth Chaiyakittiratana of *Motoring Newspaper,* and Naris Satanonchai of *Motor News Newspaper*. Their confidence in my driving ability was not enhanced by the ten minutes it took me to figure out the seat belt. "Now go slow," Naris cautioned. "I have two wives to support."

The convoy moved out and we were quickly up in the mountains. The car handled superbly. I took hairpin turns at 90kph, refusing to slow down in the slightest, in order to test the car's gripping power. It gripped. There was no reason whatsoever for Sombat to keep clutching his Buddha amulet.

We pulled off onto a dirt road to the Erawan Waterfall. Over mobile phones, drivers cracked bawdy jokes. The dirt road started out disappointingly good, but soon degenerated into a snaking, twisting, rearing, dipping, riotous torrent of mud, gullies, sump-holes, boulders, ravines, quagmires and slicks—the motoring equivalent of white-water rapids. For cross-country freaks, this was the Perfect Road.

With the old Land Rover, you would have to muscle your way out of tight spots, but now—with what felt like double the power—you just bashed through them. And with such a smooth-sailing suspension, you barely needed your seat-belt. With the old Land Rover, you always held one hand pressed up against the roof to prevent your head going through it. No need with the Jeep Cherokee. You could keep both hands on the wheel. Bad patches you would creep through in an old Land Rover were simply sailed over now. To negotiate this road at 40kph was a challenge; at 60kph, a pure thrill.

Naris took the wheel to showboat for the photographers in the car ahead, splashing through a mud pool at top speed—sending up towering sheets of brown water—then downshifting and throwing on the parking brake for a neat stop.

We emerged from a bamboo tunnel into a spectacular vista of mountain lakes, rice paddies and corn fields. Over their mobile phones, drivers warned of roadside cows, dogs, kids. Seated next to Naris, I admired his steering skills: the one-handed whipsaw through bogs, the downhill arm brace, the controlled mud glide.

Besides driving in off-road rodeos throughout Thailand, Naris had handled "Big Foots" in rallies outside Los Angeles for seven years. I was happy to let him negotiate the rest of the course, having proven that, even with a driver like me at the wheel, the Jeep Cherokee is the nearest a vehicle can get to being idiot proof.

After 103km, we took a lunch break on a scenic rise between a lake and Hoey Kamin Waterfall. Taksin gave us his verdict on the Jeep Cherokee.

"This is the best, *so* powerful, and comfortable besides." He gave us a briefing on the next stage—the five-hour jungle drive. "This will be much more difficult. Let's hope it *rains* too," he added with an evil glint in his eye.

We took off on a narrow track through the jungle, which widened and turned rocky as we climbed a mountain. We drove at a good 60kph clip along the top of ridgelines, plunged into muddy jungle again, and came out in open country—vast rolling hills like the African *veldt*, with scattered corn fields and wood farmhouses. Little kids lined the road in a Mon village to gawk and *wai*.

Then we struck the mother lode of mud: a huge, roiling, brown Mississippi of tormented ooze cascading down a steep slope, sluicing around a curve, and climbing back up a jungled ridge. Over the phone, Taksin advised us to switch to low 4X4 gear. One by one, the jeeps bucked, flopped, skidded, plunged, reared, wiggled and shimmied—this was mud surfing at its best. Naris took the rapids like a champ. Strapped in, we smashed about from side to side as he whipsawed us through—like being trapped inside a washing machine but without the regular cycles.

We were now in beautiful and hellish primal jungle. More mud torrents corkscrewed over ridges and gullies. The convoy lurched to a halt. Taksin was stuck! The second car winched him out backwards while three luckless passengers pushed from behind, coated head to foot in mud.

Some drivers speculated that Taksin had taken the rapids too fast. The trick is to negotiate the ooze at just the right speed: too fast and you pile up mud in front of you; too slow and you bog down. Taksin took the left shoulder of the road now, pioneering a new route. Naris decided to approach it at 1,500rpm—too slow. He bogged down, reversed, forwarded, reversed, and broke forward at a screaming 4,500rpm. We were out!

We bashed through more mud cataracts—four, five, six— each one longer and fiercer than the last. Sometimes Naris creeped through at 1,000rpm, other times he powered at 3,000–4,000rpm. Improvisation was the key. When the car ahead of us skidded out of three-foot deep ruts and teetered on the ridges, Naris simply chose to tiptoe atop the ridges the whole way.

By 5 p.m., we were deep in a triple-tiered National Forest Park. Overarching bamboo thickets soared skyward, blocking out the sun. Atop a rise, we saw three ridges of jungled mountains marching to the Burmese horizon. An hour later, we were still in Bandit Country as the light faded and we plunged though the Eighth Cataract. Catching his breath after a jolting, violent, side-to-side tug through the mud, Naris said, "Things could be worse."

"Yeah? How?"

"It could be raining."

"Oh."

We reached a Mon village; ran through a couple more dicey patches of road, but not as bad as before; switched finally out of 4X4; climbed straight up a mountain; crested the bedrock summit; and, in anti-skid semi-4X4, plummeted down the gravel descent road. Ten minutes later, we were back at the paved highway and civilization.

I felt like one of the survivors in *Deliverance*.

Over dinner at the Ban Rim Doi Resort, Taksin talked about plans for a week-long, four-wheel-drive rally from Kanchanaburi through the jungles of Burma to Tak. I decided to go too. Even in the rain. And one of the Chrysler people told me about a Jeep Cherokee Grand—a V-8, 5.7 liter monster.

I'll take that one.

Memories of a Great Dane

The Doctor—Einar Ammundsen

One of the perks of being a journalist is to interview a character so fascinating that you can't stop telling your friends about him for days.

Such a character was Dr. Einar Ammundsen. In early 1993, I was writing a *Manager* story about the Danes in Thailand entitled, lamely enough, "Great Danes."

The Danes have a special place in Thai history. Wary of the colonial-minded British and French, King Chulalongkorn entrusted them to develop a modern navy, police force and merchant marine. Some were even elevated to the Thai nobility.

Someone suggested I interview Dr. Ammundsen—a link to the long line of Danes who had devoted their lives in service to Thailand. The Making of an MPWe settled down in the living room—crammed with books and photographs— of his old home on Sukhumvit Soi 10, and Dr. Ammundsen told me how he had first arrived in Bangkok shortly after World War II.

"I planned to stay for five years," he recalled. "Instead, I've been here for 46. I couldn't think of a good reason to go home. . . .

"I came here by chance. A friend returned back from a voyage to Asia as a ship's surgeon, and said that he wanted to set up a practice in Bangkok. I quit my hospital job that same day. We studied tropical medicine in London for four months, and then flew to Bangkok with KLM. The trip took three days.

"At Don Muang, we asked for a hotel and were told that there wasn't one. The customs officers gave us tea and bananas before sending us to a camp for Dutch war prisoners being repatriated to Indonesia. The camp turned out to be the Oriental Hotel. We stayed there for two months. When we left the hotel, we asked if we could pay some money. We settled on a bill of one dollar a day! Afterward, we lived on Sathorn Road with a Danish sea captain. In those days, this house—this whole Sukhumvit area—was nothing but rice fields.

"We began our practice at the British Dispensary and the Bangkok Nursing Home. Thai doctors were trickling back from the war at that time, and they found the equipment and facilities here appalling. They were also burdened with the task of training a new generation of Thai doctors. There were very few specialists. I was doing things then that I'd be put in jail for now. When I look back on those times, the medical progress in Thailand has been *un-be-lievable.*

"After work, the foreign community—British, Danes, Dutch—would gather at the Sports Club. Bangkok was a village then. The international community was so small that everyone knew everyone else. Jim Thompson was a friend. . . .

"I took lessons in Thai and had no problem whatsoever adapting to the culture. I like the Thai mentality. The Danes and the Thai are both easy-going, and they have the same sense of humor—unlike the Swedes, who can be very stiff and formal.

"The Thai ambassador to Denmark and Sweden came back from the three-month stint in Stockholm and told me, 'You and the Swedes live so close to each other, but you're so different. You and I are more alike.' For the Danes, Thailand is the closest far-away country.

"Bangkok has changed radically but I've had a marvelous life here. When I first came, people said, 'You missed it. You should have seen Bangkok before the war.' But Bangkok stayed the same throughout the fifties. Field Marshal Sarit [Thanarat] really kicked things off in the early sixties."

Sometime during our conversation, I asked if I could smoke a cigarette.

"Only if you give me one," Dr. Ammundsen replied. He lit up and was suddenly racked by a vicious coughing fit. He stubbed out the cigarette regretfully, and then turned to the subject of his own health.

"To relax, I took up golf late in life," he said. "A patient once asked me why I didn't play golf, and I said that I didn't have the time. The patient replied, 'I don't mind if doctors are stupid, but not *my* doctor.' I started playing every Wednesday afternoon, and it didn't affect my work at all. I'm sorry now that I charged that patient."

On March 7, 1999, Dr. Ammundsen died of lung cancer in Denmark. Hans Einer Fugl-Svendsen, another Bangkok old hand who had known Dr. Ammussen since 1961, wrote in his obituary:

"Many will recall how worried we were when Einar developed a lung problem and was confined to the Bangkok Nursing Home, where—as he said later—they removed the part of his lung with the nicotine. Here, he left his sickroom and, adorned in a doctor's gown over his pajamas, went on his rounds to visit his patients. The matron was not amused!

"One day, the Nursing Home received a complaint from a patient about a doctor who had smoked during a consultation. Einar, as one of the directors of the hospital, was asked to reply to the complaint. This he did in typical Einar fashion. He told me that he looked at himself in the mirror and gave himself a very serious talking to. Then he wrote to the complaining patient that the doctor in question had been reprimanded."

Shootout at the FCCT

The Columnist—Bernard Trink

They're out there.

Scheming, skulking, plotting, writing enraged letters to the Post Wingebag, organizing seminars and task forces on "gender issues"—a cabal of miserable Western feminists are beavering away in Bangkok. Their tragedy is to be marooned in a fun-loving country. The target of their outrage is a little street in Bangkok known as Patpong. They don't seem to notice a legion of monster surreal Romanesque pleasure palaces—*Karaoke! Snooker! Nightclub Singers! Massage Parlor! Brothel!*—sprouting everywhere in this city. No, their laser-beamed focus is on Patpong—what they really don't like is *white* guys having a good time—and their special target is Patpong's weekly chronicler, one harmless drudge named Bernard Trink.

For over thirty years, Bernard Trink has been writing a weekly newspaper column called "The Nite Owl," covering the girlie bar scene. His crime is that he writes about prostitution from a consumer reports angle: where to find the best quality at the lowest price. For this, the feminists want to drum him out of town.

Now you don't know this because your muzzle is plunged into a beer mug in some raucous hellhole on Patpong or Soi Cowboy, but if these femi-nazis get what they want, not only will they shut down your watering hole forever, but they'll dispatch your hooker girlfriends to . . . do what? Work construction? Plant rice?

No. They've been there, done that.

Let me tell you a story. When I first came to live in Bangkok, I would frequent an *Isaan* restaurant around the corner from the Rajadamnern Boxing Stadium. One of the waitresses there was a fetching teenager named Pok—pure *ban nok*, straight out of a village in Buriram. Together we would page through a copy of *Time* magazine and she would quiz me about the photos—of Ethiopia, Cambodia, Haiti—and I would explain what was happening in all these places. Pok's eyes would well with tears. Her favorite comment: *"Naa song san!"* (What a pity!). She disappeared for a year and turned up recently for a sentimental reunion with the restaurant owner and fellow waitresses. Her schoolgirl bob had grown out long, tinted red. She clanked with gold. She wore a designer dress outfit that a year's salary as a waitress couldn't buy. Proudly, she handed me her business card: *Tokyo Bar, Thaniya Plaza*. Yes, she was surfing on the tsunami largesse of lonely Japanese businessmen.

Why does she do what she does?

For the same reason I am writing this story: money.

As a waitress, she was making 2,000 baht a month and all the *gai yang* she could eat. She makes that now in a night—an hour!—and I would no more dream of rescuing Pok from her life of prostitution than I would ask for her to rescue me from journalism.

But back to Bernard Trink. Nobody I know *likes* Trink, but everyone reads him. He does not inspire the affection of readers like, say, Roger Crutchley does. The best of Thailand's humorists—Crutch, S. Tsow, Roger Beaumont—are generally good for a half dozen laugh lines per page (Dave Barry manages that many in a paragraph, a *sentence,* but Dave Barry is possessed by the Devil). As for Bernard Trink, the times I've laughed at one of his lines—and I've been reading him for 20 years—can be counted on one finger.

His column is a farrago of self-righteous self-promotion—he never tires of telling you how honest he is—shopping tips, lame puns, lugubrious anecdotes (TIT! Manure!), and a lengthy quote from a mediocre book, concluding with "BUT

I DON'T GIVE A HOOT!" He performs a function, though, warning of ripoff bars and alerting barfly deadbeats to the latest freebie. The feminists are screaming to shut his column down: Murder the Messenger. But, hell, his tame little page is nothing compared to the heyday of the old *Bangkok World* tabloid. Twelve years ago, every Friday, old Trink had six pages devoted to hookers from Bangkok to Pattaya. Three micro-bikinied go-go dancers would be grinning furiously and dancing their butts off for the camera and the caption would read, "Three reasons for hitting the Limelight Bar. Can you spot the *katoey*?"

I say let Trink be. But nooooo, the feminist cabal got what they wanted: Trink led to a Foreign Correspondents Club of Thailand (FCCT) Wednesday night seminar, furnished with blindfold and cigarette, and hauled up before a firing squad of the PC Feminist Brigade.

Now the FCCT, to my knowledge, has hosted two feminist seminars. The first was packed with strange-looking people I had never seen before. There was a stunning six-foot blond wearing a cowboy hat who made a spectacular entrance on the arm of another woman. The panel that night were three sweet Thai *ajaans* who quietly and firmly nailed down their case for sexual equality in the Thai legal system. There were no fireworks.

Not so the second time. A smug Canadian feminist ran something called Media Watch, dedicated to stomping out the use of sexy women in advertisements. As she flipped through her slide show presentation of gorgeous babes selling stuff, the hacks along the bar—male and female—sniggered and guffawed and asked each other, "What's wrong with *that*?" Now I had resolved to keep my mouth shut, but suddenly this woman showed a slide of a six-year-old who was a dead ringer for my daughter Erika and said that the shampoo ad—"Nice and Gnarly"—was a seductive pitch for pedophilia. I rose to the defense of my daughter and concluded, "Look, I'm sorry we're all laughing at you. I'm sure this kind of feminist semiotics is all the rage in North America but we're expatriates and we just think it's silly. And your Media Watch seems suspiciously like some kind of PC Thought Police."

"I hate that term!" she snapped back. "There *is* no such thing as Political Correctness!"

"Right, and the Italians say there *is* no Mafia."

A friend of mine from California backed me up. "I'm a feminist," she told the lady. "But you've just got a dirty mind."

Still, I've been in Thailand long enough not to get pleasure out of these confrontations. I certainly have no axe to grind against women. My wife is a woman and, in the context of our marriage, I'm the whetstone. More importantly, when it comes to my three daughters, I'm a raging gut feminist. Do I want my daughters reduced to simpering, docile housewives? Hell, no! After appropriate post-graduate degrees, I expect them to plunge into the business jungle, fangs and claws aglint; to hack out a millionaire's fortune before they're thirty; and to marry obscenely rich husbands so they can support, lavishly, their old Dad in his dotage.

So what was I doing on a Wednesday night, attending a showdown between the humorless PC Feminist Brigade and the humorless Bernard Trink? Well, like the girls on Patpong, I was getting paid for it.

○ ○ ○

The FCCT is packed. Friends, male and female, I haven't seen in months are bellied up three-deep to the bar. Trink makes an unobtrusive entrance—a wizened pot-bellied gnome with trousers pulled up to his clavicle. My Californian feminist friend, Jennifer Gampell, steps up to the microphone to introduce him to the crowd—apologizing for being "a virgin moderator"—and gives Trink the stage.

"If you're really a virgin," Trink intones into the microphone, "you can ask for a lot more than a normal girl would." This gets a laugh. Trink holds up the FCCT weekly flyer. "I read this a few minutes ago. It says I've been here in Thailand since the fifties . . . . Don't tell Immigration.

"When I was invited to speak tonight, I asked, what about? They said nothing, just be yourself. Looking at this flyer now, I discover I do have a topic: Why the Nite Owl plays a vital role in the media today." Long pause. "Who, me?"

A loud laugh from the crowd. With his strong New York accent, Trink has the finely-honed timing and deadpan delivery of a Jewish comedian. He warms to his story of how he started his "entertainment" column for the now-defunct *Bangkok World*, back in 1965. Long before the advent of Patpong, he trolled the bars of Klong Toey port and discovered he had a topic.

"There were live shows even then. Women pulling snakes out of themselves. I asked them, 'How do you get it inside?' I found 13-year-old girls with more experience than me, sitting in men's laps. I looked in the faces of these girls and they were not crying inside. Nonsense! They were preparing for negotiations. One point is obvious. They do it for the money and they don't want to do anything else. There were social commentators, women, university grads, who said these girls are exploited. We have to save them, get them out of that environment. Let them be servants or paint umbrellas.

"I told the bargirls this and they laughed for thirty minutes. Asked them if they wanted to paint umbrellas, weave baskets. They said, 'You crazy? I earn 100 baht for a drink, instead of 100 a month.' The cliche on Thai TV shows is the poor prostitute crying buckets. They don't cry buckets. They want money and they'll do anything to get it."

Trink moves on to the hate mail he inspires. "The holy rollers tell me I'll burn in hell, fire, brimstone, snakes. No heaven for me. I get stacks of letters: 'You bastard, why don't you die. . .?' 'You sonofabitch, look over your shoulder in a bar and I'll be there. . .,' 'Asshole, I'll get you and your family. . .' The hate Trink crowd are the first in line to buy the weekend *Bangkok Post*. They're frustrated if it's delayed; if they don't have Trink to hate this week. If they leave the country, they still get the *Post*. I got a letter from Iceland saying, 'You scumbag.'"

Claiming that humility is not in his nature, Trink goes on to list "accomplishments" for which he never got credit. Supposedly, his column has prompted: telephone booths on New Road, movie theaters in department stores, a pedestrian overpass on New Petchaburi Road, a widening of the approach to MBK, the construction of shops and bars underneath the Expressway. . . . "Modest, I'm not."

He wraps up his talk with an estimate of a Bangkok bargirl's earnings. "She makes between 4,500–6,500 baht a month, depending if she's dancing clothed, topless or nude. But this is just pocket money. If she's taken out every night of the month, she's making 75,000 baht, plus drink tips, tax free."

His estimate of the number of hookers in Thailand: 300,000. "That's 1% of the female population and that's what I'm writing about," he concludes. "If you want to be angry at me, go ahead. But I'm not writing about the other 99%."

Bernard Trink gets a round of applause. It's question time now and the audience braces itself gleefully for the feminist counterattack. And . . . nothing. Of the twenty people who pose questions, only three are women.

"You're always writing about the same bars," one guy notes. "Do you feel that you're not cut out for the job anymore, that you're too old?"

"No."

"In Australia, a prostitute costs 700 dollars," another guy follows up. "There seems to be a question of supply and demand. Would you care to address this question?"

"No."

Finally, Jennifer Gampell asks, "As a responsible journalist, don't you feel you have an obligation to inform the public about AIDS?"

Trink replies that there is a theory that HIV does not necessarily lead to AIDS. "There is no AIDS on Patpong. Bargirls are a high risk group, so why not? Tell me where and I'll go there tonight. I try to give both sides of the AIDS argument." He holds up a book by a doctor claiming that heterosexual sex is not linked to AIDS. "You be the judge."

A half dozen questions later, a woman journalist challenges Trink. "You say that there's no proof of an HIV link to AIDS. Why don't you apply yourself as a newsman to investigate, instead of being a conduit for any misinformation that crosses you desk?"

"I'd have to give up what I do. You have your belief. I try to present all views."

The journalist sits down, muttering, "Like the Nazi view of the Holocaust?"

The questions taper to a halt. No fireworks. Trink concludes, "I may be older than the hills, but seeing 13 naked dancers keeps me going." The crowd has been drifting away.

Afterwards at the bar, a journalist tells me that six of her friends left out of boredom. "There's no reason to get up for what the old duffer was saying. When I first came here, I might have squashed him, but I've been in Thailand for three and a half years and what's the point? I mean, why bother?"

That seemed to be the consensus amid the seasoned Bangkok hands, and among the women who work in journalism, advertising, TV and radio. At the FCCT, for that night anyway, there was just no base of PC airheads to get thrown into a tizzy.

Maybe they're *not* out there.

How the South Was Won
The Soldier—Kitti Ratanachaya

Kitti Ratanachaya first saw combat as a 27-year-old lieutenant. He was commanding a platoon in "Operation Peninsular"— a massive Thai-Malaysian sweep of Communist Party of Malaya (CPM) jungle hideouts on the border from Sadao to Betong. The year was 1963.

Twenty years later, in the Banthad Mountains of his home province, Surat Thani, he was a regimental commander in the fierce battle that destroyed Camp 508—headquarters of the Communist Party of Thailand (CPT). In between, he served a combat tour in Vietnam and fought Muslim separatists in the Deep South. Through it all, he was never wounded.

"I was lucky," he admits as he relaxes in the Bangkok clubhouse of the Royal Thai Army golf course.

In 1989, as deputy commander of the Fourth Army, then Major-General Kitti talked the 2,000-strong CPM out of the jungle. A year later, he accepted the surrender of the last 251 insurgents of the CPT. Only a decade earlier, the CPT had fielded over 3,000 armed guerrillas in a broad swathe of South Thailand.

So what went right?

"The experience of the Thai army in fighting the communists proved that if you treated them like enemies, you'd never win," Lieutenant-General Kitti says. "With guerrilla troops, the situation is like a piece of wood floating in the sea: it just rises and falls with the tide. The army made a mistake with big search-and-destroy missions. After a long study, they changed their strategy. Negotiation is the best way. If you make insurgents wear a suit and tie and sit at the table, you've already won."

The history of the rise and fall of both the CPT and the CPM bears the general out. In 1965, when the CPT began armed operations against the Thai government, their insurgents in the South numbered 250 in 17 bands scattered through the mountainous jungle of Nakhon Si Thammarat, Surat Thani and Phattalung. Three years later, they numbered 400, and by the end of 1970, over 1,000, spreading south into Trang, Songkhla and Satun.

"Due to the inability of the Southern Region Army commander [Major-General Cherm Preutsayachiwa] to understand the nature of the problem, very little effort was made to deal with local communist activities," writes General Saiyud Kerdphol in his book, *The Struggle for Thailand*.

Founder of the Communist Suppression Operations Command (CSOC), General Saiyud, and like-minded generals, advocated a counter-insurgency program of rural development and armed village volunteers working in close cooperation with civilian officials and military forces.

But from 1968 to 1970, the army decided to go its own way—with massive search-and-destroy sweeps. These served only to drive more farmers into the arms of the insurgents.

Harsh suppression measures, especially in Phattalung, where suspect communists were burned in oil drums—the infamous "red tanks"—caused guerrilla ranks to swell to 1,800 by 1973. After the 1976 Thammasat University massacre, Southern Thai students flocked to the CPT, bringing the insurgency to a peak strength of 3,000 in 1979.

"In the South, corruption by police and government officials was the main reason for people to flee into the jungle," observes Lieutenant-General Kitti. "If your strategy is just to kill communists, this is wrong. That's what happened in Phattalung."

The turning point in the battle for the South came in April 1980, when Prime Minister Prem Tinsulanond issued his famous "Directive 65/23," which called for political measures to be given priority over military operations in combating the CPT. Student leaders were the first to take advantage of amnesty terms and emerge from the jungle. More surrenders followed after General Chuan Wanarat captured the bunkered jungle base of Camp 508 in Surat Thani.

Prem, a native of Songkhla, took a special interest in the South, transferring corrupt police and civilian officials out of the region, and replacing them with hand-picked people known for their honesty. The South, formerly a dumping ground for the greedy and inept, now became a proving ground for the ambitious and efficient.

In 1982, Prem appointed protege and fellow Southerner, Han Linanond, as Fourth Army commander. Lieutenant-General Han embarked upon a whirlwind pacification program called *Tai Rom Yen* ("Cool Shade in the South"). This combined the open hand of amnesty with the iron fist of combat offensives.

"General Han had the right idea," says Lieutenant-General Kitti. "I enjoyed working for him. I was the one who started up the People's Resistance Against Communism (PRAC) program. The concept was to get villagers involved in their own defense, with the ideal being Ban Rajan—the village that had courageously resisted a Burmese invasion during the Ayuthaya period. The communist strategy was for the jungle to surround the town. With rural development, we made the town surround the jungle."

By 1985, the CPT was a spent force, reduced to a couple hundred die-hard holdouts. Kitti, now commander of the Fifth Infantry Division, turned his attention to the CPM—Thailand's oldest insurgency.

Founded in 1930, the CPM played a major role in resistance to the Japanese occupation of Malaya during World War II. In 1948, under the leadership of Chin Peng, 12,000 CPM insurgents opened guerrilla warfare against the British. As the war turned against them, the CPM retreated to bases along the Thai border in Narathiwat, Yala, Pattani and Songkhla. For forty years, three regiments of 2,600 CPM cadres held out against combined operations by the Thai and Malaysian military.

As Lieutenant-General Kitti recalls in his book, *Taming the Southern Fire*, "Thailand and Malaysia were unable to defeat the Malaysian communist guerrillas outright in warfare as the latter were familiar with the terrain, skilled in jungle warfare, and skilled in hiding and retreating—employing Mao Tze-Tung's war tactics of 'When you come, we hide; when you stop, we harass; when you are in trouble, we attack; when you run, we follow.' It is pointless mentioning development in the Thai-Malaysian border region as there was little chance for any to take place with the area in a constant state of war."

Every year, Kitti's troops were taking sixty casualties from mines and booby traps alone. In 1985, he had Prem's "Order 66/23" translated into Chinese and distributed to all CPM units.

"Our policy was twofold," he explains. "We offered them the chance to come out of the jungle and help develop the nation. The alternative was relentless heavy suppression."

Two years later, 631 members of a dissident CPM faction surrendered to the governors of Songkhla and Yala provinces. This left Kitti, now deputy commander of the Fourth Army, to deal with the 2,000 cadres still loyal to Chin Peng.

"It was a question of negotiations from the bottom up," he remembers. "We first contacted CPM sympathizers, then low-level cadres, then the leadership itself—which met secretly with me many times in Hat Yai. I met too with the Royal Malaysian Army, asking them to take part in negotiations, but they said they had no political policy for this. So I continued on alone."

In 1989, the Malaysians had a change of heart. Prime Minister Dr. Mahathir instructed Inspector Datuk Abdul

Rahim Bin Mohd of the Royal Malaysian Police's Special Branch, to open negotiations with the CPM. Rebuffed by the CPM, he was told to contact Major-General Kitti.

"I realized that this was a golden opportunity to include Malaysia in the negotiations as, after all, they were the real enemies of the communist guerrillas," Kitti comments. "If all three sides could agree, then hostilities could come to an end, and a genuine, permanent peace could come to the border region."

By now, Kitti had already met with the acting CPM secretary-general, Chang Ling Yan, at a Hat Yai hotel.

"The CPM at first didn't believe in our sincerity," recalls Lieutenant-General Kitti. "We had to prove to them that we were sincere and would treat them with respect."

Chang Ling Yan reported that the CPM had agreed to end hostilities, but would need to confer with Secretary-General Chin Peng, who had been exiled to China since 1961.

Together with CPM leaders, Kitti's invaluable aide, Colonel Akanit Muensaweat, traveled five times to Guangzhou to meet with Chin Peng. The party leader eventually acceded to the idea of disbanding his army, and sent his representative, Madame Zainon, to confer with the CPM in their jungle bases. On February 2nd, 1989, she and CPM local leaders met with Kitti and Malaysian representatives for the first of five tripartite peace talks in Phuket.

Much of the early negotiations involved torturous semantics to avoid loss of face for the veteran CPM cadres.

"The word 'surrender' cannot be found in the CPM dictionary," stated Chang Ling Yan at the time. The word finally agreed upon was to "dissolve" the party. Similarly, the CPM would not "hand over" their weapons, but did agreed to "destroy" them. A considerable amount of haggling was devoted to the financial terms of resettlement.

"In negotiations, you must know when you should move on, and when you should step back," Lieutenant-General

Kitti observes. "When talks would reach an impasse, I'd call for a coffee break and then move between the two groups. At night, I'd have both groups mix socially—with the help of plenty of whiskey. There was a piano in the hotel lounge, and I'd get the Malaysians to sing a song, and the CPM to sing another."

By the fourth meeting in Phuket, Kitti felt confident enough to invite Chin Peng to make a surprise trip to Thailand. Accompanied by Colonel Akanit, Chin Peng arrived at Don Muang Airport to be greeted by Kitti, who welcomed him as "*pee*" [older brother], and invited him to stay at his family's house. He did not tell his wife the identity of the mystery visitor.

"I didn't spend that much time with him, but Chin Peng came across as a gentleman: intelligent, polite and straight-forward," Lieutenant-General Kitti says. "He's a patriot who helped to fight the Japanese. He worked for the welfare of Malaysia, not China. I still see him from time to time. In fact, I had dinner with him recently in Hat Yai."

In Phuket, the Malaysians were shocked by the appearance of their legendary *bete noir*.

"Colonel Akanit told me that Chin Peng was very cheerful, whistling on his way to the hotel," Lieutenant-General Kitti recalls. Negotiations were swiftly wrapped up, and a peace treaty was signed in Hat Yai on December 2nd, 1989. "I was granted my wish to have the peace treaty signed before His Majesty's birthday," Kitti says.

Six hundred CPM cadres, many of them elderly, returned to Malaysia. The remaining 1,600 CPM were resettled along the Thai border region. The top leadership, including Chin Peng, now lives peacefully in Hat Yai.

For his crucial role in ending the forty-year insurgency, Lieutenant-General Kitti was knighted by the King of Malaysia as a *Dato*—one of only two Thai so honored.

In 1990, Kitti turned his attention to the last insurgency in Thailand—the Muslim separatists of the Malay-speaking provinces of Yala, Pattani and Narathiwat. In 1980, two allied organizations—the Pattani United Liberation Front (PULO) and the Barisan Revolusi Nasional (BRN)—had fielded 1,000 guerrillas against the Thai army, but after a decade of suppression and surrenders, their forces were reduced to just 120 active fighters. They survived on subsidies supplied by several Middle-Eastern countries.

As Fifth Division commander, Kitti had taken the unprecedented step of setting up a coordinating group of respected Muslim leaders to help tackle problems in the border area. Key Islamic figures were named as his personal advisors, and their opinions were sought whenever conflicts arose over religious issues.

"This way we could avoid tension in the area and be able to nip any problems in the bud," says Kitti, who sided with the Muslim community when Thai officials tried to ban the wearing of traditional *hiyap* head-dress by female students. "We have to be open-minded and learn to respect the difference between our brothers and sisters who are Muslims," he stated at the time.

In mid-1993, Kitti, soon to be Fourth Army commander, dispatched Colonel Akanit to Cairo to meet with PULO leader, Tunku Bilor Kortornilor. Another meeting was held in Damascus a year a later. Colonel Akanit was accompanied this time by a respected Thai Muslim diplomat. A third meeting was scheduled in Sweden in 1995, but was aborted when Kitti was removed from his command in late 1994 and kicked upstairs to an inactive post in Bangkok.

There had never been any love lost between the popular Southern general and army commander, Wimol Wongwanich. A similar fate happened to General Han Leenanond, removed from the Fourth Army command in 1984 by General Arthit

Kamlang-ek. The irony is that army politics are often more vicious than communist insurgencies. The new Fourth Army commander, Lieutenant-General Parnthep Puwanartnurak, reversed Kitti's initiatives.

"Akanit is now a 'special colonel' at Fourth Army headquarters," reports Kitti. "General Parnthep doesn't like him, and he doesn't agree with my policies. I'm in the same position as General Han now. I have a high rank but no work to do. General Han resigned and went into politics.

"I'm interested in politics but there are no rules there. I've been in the military for 35 years. I believe in an honor system, and my reputation and good name. I could lose all this by entering politics. I'm just waiting to retire. I plan to work for royal projects at the Chulaporn Institute. Right now, I have the time to play golf and to write."

Fine Threads

The Silk Queen—Khanitha Akaranitikul

The upper end of Suriwong Road is Silk Row. Along with a dozen smaller stores, here you will find the emporiums of the leading names in Thai silk: Jim Thompson and Khanitha.

Waiting on the second floor of the atrium of Khanitha's palatial showroom, I mistake the woman approaching with coffee for the secretary—because Khanitha Akaranitikul looks 15 years younger than her forty-something.

Born in Rachaburi, Khanitha attended high school in Bangkok and was married right after she graduated. "That was the end of my education, except for short courses in English and clothing design," she says. But a future in a traditional housewife role did not appeal to the young Khanitha. "Screaming," is her code word for boredom and frustration.

"After the birth of my first daughter, I started screaming," she explains. "I was 22 when I started up my first Thai silk workshop in the Indra Hotel. I had two sewing machines, and my staff were two seamstresses and a pattern maker. I was the designer. Two years later, I opened up my own store. I have four now: the one here on Suriwong, and three others at the Regent, Siam Center, and River City.

"I do almost everything: sales, advertising, designing, even sweeping the floor. The administrative end is handled by my husband, a former law professor at Khon Kaen University. I'd say that 70% of my customers are tourists, the remainder Thai. Half my production is exported: 60% to Europe, 20% to the US, and 20% to Japan, Australia and elsewhere.

"When I opened my first shop, tourists were just beginning to come to Bangkok in large numbers. They wanted to take something home with them, and Thai silk was a natural gift. As more and more tourists came, the name of my shop spread

by word of mouth. My first international clients actually came to *me*—arriving in Bangkok specifically to order my silk line. Then I started advertising, using international models.

"What I've done is change the image of Thai silk. Before, it was considered old-fashioned, traditional, and ethnic. I changed this by designing Thai silk for up-to-date fashions—a young, modern image. Twice a year I travel abroad—New York, Paris, Milan—to check out new fashion trends and meet buyers. We're the leading exporter of Thai silk garments. Jim Thompson leads in terms of material.

"I started out like Jim Thompson, making contact with the weavers. At peak, I employed 200–300 weavers, mostly in Bangkok. Some still weave silk by hand looms; others have machines to finish the fabric. I show them the colors and patterns. Twice a year, I have a new collection but I don't bother with fashion shows. They're too time-consuming for only a few minutes exposure.

"In 1992, I opened a Thai silk factory in Samut Prakan, but it wasn't the best timing, what with all the political problems in Thailand. At first we had 400 employees but I now keep only 100. The recession has hit the business hard. This is a problem when you're sticking to one product. I'm working now at combining Thai silk with natural fibers like linen and cotton. They're cooler to wear."

Like most people in Bangkok, Khanita's life is dominated by the traffic. She gets up at 6 a.m. each morning at her home on Sukhumvit Soi 11 in order to reach work at nine. After work, she goes to a gym to work out with weights and "take out my madness." She also swims and plays tennis and golf—traveling to courses in Hua Hin, Chiang Mai, Phuket and Pattaya. Her trips abroad are short, and packed with business meetings.

"I enjoy the business. It's *sanuk*. I enjoy the decision making and thinking up new ways of creating beauty. I feel a great sense of satisfaction when I see customers wearing my designs. I was watching the Miss Universe contest in Mexico once, when I recognized one of my outfits on a member of the audience. Nobody else knew, but I did. You can see the results of your work.

"My oldest daughter may take after me. She's in New York in her third year at the Parsons School of Design. My second daughter, now 19, is at ABAC [Assumption Business Administration College]. My son, who's 16, is somewhat naughty. I had to make hard choices as I built up my business, and my one regret is that I left my children with the maids too much—with not enough of my love and attention. I wish I could have given my children a more normal life."

Just on cue, her 19-year old daughter, in ABAC uniform, comes running up the stairs behind the leash of a slavering springer spaniel. The dog is so excited that it promptly wets the floor.

Khanitha laughs in exasperation. "That dog belonged to my elder daughter in New York. She found it hard to take care of in an apartment, taking it for walks in the snow. So it's mine now."

Returning to the silk business, Khanitha says that her major concern is a lack of responsibility on the part of her workers. "This gets me screaming. There's high competition for local talent. How to stimulate motivation and loyalty? This is something I'll have to address in the future. We need more concentration on training. We have to stay alert to the competition or we'll lose control to outsiders. Vietnam, for example, is entering the silk trade in a big way, setting up new factories. We may have to move further upwards from our upper-middle niche in the market."

Does she ever think about doing something else?

"I wish I could have stopped working yesterday. I'd like to slow down somewhat. Maybe I'll semi-retire. Live on an island or a mountainside." She rolls her eyes at the panting spaniel at her feet. "With my dog."

Queens of Rome

The Drag Artists

I love black girls. I've always loved black girls. My first girlfriend was a black Puerto Rican. The first woman I slept with was a Jamaican. The first woman I lived with was a Fula from Sierra Leone. My girlfriend in Brazil was a green-eyed *mulata* from Recife. My wife is a dark-skinned, half-Malay Southern Thai.

So when a brochure landed on my desk advertising a beauty pageant at the Rome Club, I was immediately sucked in by the cover: a striking picture of a dusky, busty *luk kreung* (half-Thai, half-foreign) wearing a spangled bodice and a tiara. Only when I read the fine-print did I discover that the contestants for the "Queen of Rome" crown were not anatomically correct. But what the hell.

The Rome Club on Silom Soi 4 is Bangkok's premier gay discotheque. "We have always been the pioneer in Bangkok," explains owner, Manuel Pineda, sipping coffee on the club's terrace. "We were the first disco, the first videotheque and the first terrace cafe. I travel around the world twice a year getting new design ideas."

The Rome Club hit a bad patch when Manuel was in London for cancer chemotherapy. The nadir was struck when the temporary management banned homosexuals—a bit like the Apollo Theater in Harlem banning blacks.

"I want to apologize for that," Manuel states firmly. "The Rome Club is against all kinds of discrimination. When I returned, we closed the club down for a year and a half, spent 15 million baht in renovations—designed by my partner, Tira—and we're now open again for business."

Tonight's "Queen of Rome" pageant is the first at the club in ten years. Manuel explains that the queens take it very

seriously, but they had to stop the shows because, "The crowds, the screaming, it just became too much. But I decided that the club's reopening demanded a special celebration." Hence tonight's show.

The house is packed. An S & M show featuring two muscle men and a leather-corsetted drag dominatrix gets the crowd warmed-up. Amid a musical fanfare, smoke and strobe lights, MC "Day" takes the stage to launch the beauty contest. The panel of judges includes the current Miss Thailand, and the first-prize is 40,000 baht.

The gowned and sequined contestants—36 queens from all over Thailand—sashay down the catwalk. Some work the seductively female angle; some the comically outrageous. One long-haired beauty, attired in a skin-tight black leather mini-skirt, pirouettes gracefully at the end of her turn, wiggles her magnificent ass, and casts a coy glance over her shoulder, sending a bolt of lust through every male in the room.

Many contestants flaunt brand-new breasts and high-pitched voices to match. One smugly confesses during her interview with MC Day that she has had surgery to make her a "*pooying riap roi*"—a proper lady.

Raunchy camp and vamp dominate the show, however, and only two subdued beauties make it to the final five: an elegant Audrey Hepburn lookalike and a virginal blonde in a bouffant wedding-cake gown. The three other finalists are clad in a 25kg chain-mail dress; lipstick-red hotpants; and a leopardskin-and-black lingerie ensemble topped with a birdcage bonnet.

Crowned "Queen" is Audrey Hepburn—alias "Miss Wat"—a 25-year-old make-up artist, resplendent in a slinky sheath, an explosive aviary of white feathers, and a generous supply of glitter.

What will she do with her prize money?

"Open my own beauty shop," she replies sweetly. "Or maybe buy my boyfriend a motorcycle."

Market Forces

The Aranyapathet Market Traders And Buyers

Was last year a tough one for you? Dividends slashed? Bonus canceled? Struggling to make ends meet?

Join the army of bargain hunters at the border market of Aranyapathet. The four-hour train ride from Bangkok's Hualampong Station to Aranyaphathet costs less than the start-up fare for a city taxi.

From the station, a motorcycle-*tuk tuk* will whisk you the final 8km to the Cambodian border. The newly-paved road to the market is a mob scene of pickup trucks. License plates read Lopburi, Sisaket, Ratburi, Ubon, Korat, Chonburi, Samut Sakhon, Rayong, Supanburi, Chayasen, Nakhon Nayok, Kanchanaburi. The largest number of pickups, however, come from nearby Prachinburi and Chachoengsao—the sites for a dozen industrial estates. Come payday, factory workers are out in force, their ranks boosted by border-based soldiers and fruit plantation owners. Passenger cars arrive mainly from the Bangkok area, including meter-taxis.

Two hundred meters from the border, the road branches in two. A fleet of 18-wheel trucks loaded with Siam Cement bags heads straight for Cambodia. The pickups turn left into the market of concrete sheds that march in ranks toward the horizon. A parking lot tollbooth charges for cars and trucks, while everything else on wheels is allowed in free. Four hundred vehicles cover barely a quarter of the vast lot.

"This was once just a big puddle of mud," observes Usanee Ekkarot, a part-time petty trader from Prachinburi. "And the market was just a tent city. Now that the government has built concrete sheds, the market has tripled in size. Of all the border markets—Hat Yai, Sungai Golok, Ranong—this is the most open. There are no crackdowns [on smuggling]."

The market looks like an army camp. White concrete barracks are in four ranks, ten-deep, with 15 shops on each side—for a total of 600. Each shop is the size of a garage with a steel door to match. Roofs are identical pantile.

At 10:30 a.m., the market has been open for two hours and is already packed. It will grow even more crowded until closing time at 3:30 p.m. Thai shoppers stream in from the parking lot, while Cambodian vendors push handcarts from the Thai customs post. Cambodian men seem to favor army shirts; the women, straw hats with flowers. Child beggars swarm through the aisles, many with small auxiliary beggars on their hips.

"This isn't like the market on the Malaysian border," continues Usanee. "There, the main items are electronics, videos, camera equipment. Here, the goods are simple: toys from China, handicrafts from Vietnam, used clothes from America. Ninety percent of the vendors are Cambodian. The 10% who are Thai sell upscale products—mobile phones, karaoke video players—for the Cambodians to resell over the border."

Used clothes fill nearly half the shops. According to Usanee, Cambodian traders bid at auctions for large lots at Cambodian ports, then transport the goods to Aranyaphatet.

"Last time, I bought leather jackets for 300 baht apiece," she says. "Then I sold them in Prachinburi for 700 baht; others in Songkhla for 1,200 baht. Children's clothes cost as little as ten baht. I resold some kids stuff in Songkhla for 100 baht. I also deal in soap and make-up."

The used clothing seems to come from everywhere. Japanese suits sell for as little as 100 baht, and are even cheaper if bought in bulk. Canadian uniform jackets—customs, air force, forest ranger—are priced at only 80 baht. Malaysian raincoats go for the same price, or 60 baht in bulk. Cambodian army shirts are a bargain at 65 baht.

There are fur-lined parkas and Chicago Bears NFL jackets. A real American air force leather jacket sells for 350 baht. The collar label advises the wearer of the provisions of the Geneva POW accord. "You are required to give only name, rank and serial number."

Other shops sell second-hand curtains, rugs, shoes and stuffed toys. A friend of Usanee is buying up Chinese "Joanna" sunglasses for 80 baht. He will resell them to his co-workers at a Prachinburi paper mill for 250 baht. He is also on the lookout for Chinese "Lwin" guitars, on sale for 320 baht. The more upmarket "Adam" electric guitar costs 2,400 baht. A 250 baht "Yongmei" electric organ can be sold for triple the price in Bangkok.

Toys are a big item. One shop sells a Chinese knockoff of a Barbie doll—"Donna" the rock star, complete with guitar and costume change—for 35 baht. For the same price, you can pick up a "House of Cheer and Fun" doll's house or a "Happy Wheels" set of ten Chinese Matchbox metal cars. A complete "Union Express" train set, adorned with American flags, can be yours for 250 baht.

An especially popular toy is the "Talking Parrot"—a lifelike bird perched outside dozens of shops—which repeats whatever you say three times. Prices quoted vary between 160–200 baht. Inform a vendor that another shop has offered a lower price for the parrot and receive the inevitable reply: "Good. Go and buy it there then."

Plastic flowers, lamps, clocks, belts, perfumes, flashlights, tools, hubcaps, steering wheel locks, scissors, combs, nail polish, costume jewelry, umbrellas, running shoes, calculators, video games, karaoke tapes . . . Cigarettes and whiskey are about the only items not displayed for sale. However, roving vendors are happy to oblige with cartons of "West" Cambodian filter cigarettes for 100 baht, or genuine Marlboros for 200 baht. Police loudspeakers warn against adulterated Scotch.

Large, plastic cigarette lighters are sold in lots of 50 for 130 baht. Bronze, Vietnamese lighters—cannons, tanks, pistols, sports cars—sell for 60 baht. Switchblades and flick-knives go for 100 baht. For 250 baht you can buy Vietnamese paintings of the Holy and Thai royal families—again, priced lower in bulk.

An "American Commando 100% Top Quality Hammock" is on sale for 50 baht—made in Vietnam of course. There are also Vietnamese hats, mats, baskets and porcelain vases. Bronzeware—Buddha statues, bowls, candlesticks, elephants, horses, ox-carts—sell for around 200 baht. A Vietnamese rosewood and mother-of-pearl chair must be the market's most expensive product at 18,000 baht.

At the corners of the barracks are the busy, Thai-owned *kway-tiao* shops, which are licensed to print money. These double-sized shops rent for 13,000 baht a month. The ordinary shops are 6,000 baht. For those who cannot afford these rents, there are the remains of the old tent city to the north of the market.

Foodstuffs form the bulk of the produce offered in the tent city. Apples are eight baht. Pepper, garlic, peanuts, honey, dried fish, and other assorted herbs, spices, fruits and vegetables are all priced at a fraction of what you would pay at a Bangkok market.

Usanee snaps up two bales of dried squid and frog skin. Folk medicines are particularly popular. Bear bile is 250 baht; porcupine stomach, 60 baht; starfish, 50 baht each; tiger teeth, 250 baht; and baby deer horns, 400 baht.

By 2 p.m., the crowds start to thin out. In the parking lot, pickup trucks bulge with black garbage bags packed with goods.

A Thai woman from Aranyaphatet is selling fried squid from a pushcart. "Everything's expensive today," she comments. "You should come back on a weekday."

"These Cambodian people are so stupid," adds another Thai lady, who is pounding *somtam*. "They pay when they bring things into Thailand, then pay again when they go back with Thai things. Thailand is like a tiger that just sleeps and waits for Cambodian people to bring meat."

On the train back to Bangkok, experienced traders bring out their Philips screwdrivers. With these, they unscrew wall panels and ceiling fittings, behind which they hide bags of Marlboro cartons. The mood is festive. Vendors of *Mekhong* whiskey and *Singha* beer do a roaring trade.

The 'Brain Gain'

The Ex-expats

When Prime Minister Chuan Leekpai—during his first term of office—encouraged an audience of Thai businessmen in Los Angeles to come home, he was a few years behind the times. The movement back to Thailand started over a decade ago, when the country really began to boom.

No one knows exactly how many Thais returned—or relocated again after the bust of 1997—or even how many are living abroad now. Estimates of the Thai population in the US alone run as high as 300,000. Anecdotal evidence abounds, however, that Thai expatriates have flocked home in large numbers.

"I think the reverse migration began in the late eighties," says Bruce Martin, managing director of the Leo Burnett advertising company. "When I first began recruiting staff, maybe one in a hundred had been educated or lived aboard. Now it's more like one in two. I hired a woman with an MBA in direct marketing. Only a few years ago, there was no such thing in Thailand."

One such returnee is Gessanie Skuldist, creative director at Ogilvy & Mather. She spent seven years in the US before returning to Bangkok in 1987.

"After getting my MA in communications design from Pratt Institute, I worked for Ogilvy & Mather in New York," she recalls. "If you can make it in New York, you can make it anywhere. I can make it here—and faster too.

"I came back to Bangkok for a visit and saw that there were better opportunities here for my career. Also, my English is not perfect, while my Thai is. Another reason was that my husband, a photographer, found the competition very stiff in New York. He's opened his own studio in Bangkok and has been very successful.

"I started off with a Thai salary, not an expat one. At first, this was 50% less than what I was making in New York. Now it's 25% more. But there's real job satisfaction here, and much more responsibility. There's a technology lag, and you have to solve problems by yourself—improvise solutions in printing and photography—whereas in New York you have a large team of specialists. In New York, I was limited to just creative work, but now my responsibilities have expanded into the managerial side as well. Things like billings, budget and expenses.

"My first year, I went back and forth between Bangkok and New York, but now I have no regrets. All in all, life in Bangkok is better, but there are so many things to do and see in New York. It was exciting: walking the streets, browsing in the shops, sitting in sidewalk cafes in Soho watching the crowds go by.

"Here in Bangkok, you don't do much walking. You're much more alert in New York too—you have to be, because of the muggers. That's another advantage of Bangkok. But Bangkok and New York are similar in that there's a lot to do at night—all night. There are more restaurants now, more places to hang out. Some of my Thai friends in New York have already come back to Bangkok, and others are thinking about it."

Before returning to Thailand to work for Leo Burnett, information systems manager Pichate Pitanpitayarat lived in the US for nine years. With a degree in accounting from Thammasat University, he had continued on to Mankato State University in Minnesota, earning a master's degree in math and computers. From there, he went to work in Chicago.

"People in Chicago were always asking if it was cold enough for me. I'd tell them, 'I just came from Minnesota, where the cold can't get any worse.' Actually, this was a suburb of Chicago, a half hour away by car. Chicago itself was dangerous, and I avoided riding the subway and the el. I lived in Oakbrook Terrace, a bedroom community that was converting to a business center. I loved it there. The air was clean, the people were friendly, and there was a Thai temple just five miles away.

"There were three of us Thai friends who went to the same school, the same computer courses, and had the same jobs in the same company. Montong and Thannasan left before me, though. They both got married and had kids, and wanted them to grow up in Thailand and not be *farangs*. Plus they got a bit homesick.

"Why did I come back? Basically, my career was not up to the point I wanted it to be. My friends had come back too, and I didn't have much of a social life. I came back to Bangkok for the first time in nine years and I was shocked. The city had changed so much: traffic everywhere, pollution, over-crowding. I got lost. There were new buildings, and even new roads like Rama IX and Rachada. It was almost a brand-new city, but my old friends from school and the neighborhood were the same as they used to be. I thought I'd feel alien, but no, I felt right at home again. It was like I'd never left. My family thought I'd gone forever, so it was an emotional reunion. I live at home with my mother, which is only right after all these years.

"In the US, I went from programmer to systems analyst to project leader—purely technical. Here, I'm head of the whole information systems department, with much more re-sponsibility. I do everything in the department: management, bills, finances, drawing up the scope of the job, and budgeting. I'm as excited by this job as I was with my first one straight out of college. It's challenging and fun; something new every day.

"I've had to become Thai again. Take humor, for instance. Americans joke about everything to everybody. Here, people were shocked that I'd joke around with parents, elders, superiors. They thought I opened up more than I should.

"I'm making 80% of what I did in the States but, with the cost of living, it comes out the same. I don't pay rent, but my car costs twice as much. I loved life in the US. People were nice and very easy to get along with. You're free to do anything—nobody cares. On the other hand, nobody cares about you."

Ruangroj Supanpong, director and general manager of MHE Demag, a manufacturer of industrial cranes, is a member of an earlier generation of Thai expatriates. After graduating from St. Joseph's School, he accompanied a cousin to Stuttgart to study German in 1963. He would spend seven years working and studying before returning to Thailand as an engineer.

"Did I like Germany? You'd have to separate the answer into compartments. I liked their way of working; the toughness of it. I didn't like the social life. I had some good friends in Germany but, for the most part, the people are cool toward you, and there's always some distance. On the other hand, once they accept you, you can rely on them forever as good, firm friends.

"In general, though, it was hard for me as a student. You'd go to rent a room and the landlord would slam the door in your face. The same with buses: you'd run up and the driver would slam the door.

"We were accepted in the school because the academics were broad-minded, but the working class—especially those over forty—were hopelessly closed. They don't like outsiders, especially of a different race. Their attitude was, 'Why are you here? Why aren't you in your own country?'

Some of the Thai medical students who married German girls stayed on, but almost all of the engineers and those in the technical professions came back. There are three reasons for this," Ruangroj holds up three fingers. "One, personal: the Thai don't like the social scene. Two, professional: you can advance only to a certain point and there's a cap on your career because there are plenty of Germans to take professional jobs. And, three," he grins broadly, ticking off a third finger, "they don't want you."

Chatra Vasikut, management information systems manager for Siam Occidental Electrochemical Company, had a more pleasant experience during her 12-year stay in Texas.

"I was born in Bangkok but, when I was 14, I went to India to attend a convent school in the Himalayas," she recalls. "I came back to Bangkok with a college degree in psychology. After two years, I went to stay with my sister in Dallas. I studied computer science for seven years at North Texas State in Denton, twenty miles north of Dallas. Then I worked for four more years at ITS Corporation, a software house, writing programs for the oil and gas industry, and then—with the crash of oil prices—for insurance companies.

"I loved Texas. I loved the cowboys, country music, dancing. But socially, there wasn't as much to do as in Bangkok. Saturdays, I'd go shopping. Sundays, I'd watch sports on TV with my husband. I'm a big Dallas Cowboys fan. I came back to Thailand because my father was ill.

"My first year back was tough, adapting to the culture. There's a great emphasis on appearances, outside presentation, and dressing up. You're always aware of the community around you. You have to respect elders and not answer back. The Thais can't accept confrontation; can't tell people frankly what's wrong with them. I've had to learn to talk my way around problems.

"Thailand is ten years behind the US in computers. I've had to change people's minds about technology. Kids in the

US know all about computers and kids here are catching up. The difficulty is in middle management—they really don't understand computers. I have to communicate as much as I can in layman's terms, not technical ones. The problem is that a lot of computer science words are English. There are simply no Thai equivalents. People don't understand this. They think that I'm just showing off my English.

"Even now, after five years, I'm still only making 80% of my former stateside salary. On the other hand, my home in Banglamphu is only a five minute walk from my office. That's like having it all.

"I do have some regrets about leaving the US. I miss the independence of living in the States. It's just you alone, or with your husband—you decide things and you do them. Here, your parents, and even your aunts and uncles all get into the act. There, you decide by yourself. The disadvantage, of course, is when you need someone to help.

"I miss the Dallas Cowboys too. I always followed them on TV and sometimes in the stadium, which was very exciting. My biggest regret is that I never attended a Super Bowl."

Chira Hongladarom, executive director of Thammasat's Human Resources Institute, has researched the Thai expatriate phenomenon in the US. In his most recent study, he found that over half (56%) were employed in the fields of engineering and computers; a quarter in management and business administration; and the remainder in science, medicine, education and agriculture. Seventy percent retained Thai nationality. Two thirds were married to Thai spouses, 10% to Americans, and the remainder single or divorced. One third were making more than US$36,000 a year.

"We found that people were willing to take a salary cut to come back to Thailand, provided such things as legal status, education, housing and fair job advancement were taken into account," comments Dr. Chira.

"It's up to the government now to expand the program to attract Thai talent back to Thailand. Taiwan and Korea have been very successful in attracting people back who were lost to the 'brain drain.' The Korean Development Institute, for example, searched out the best economists, and they also found people to develop their chemical industry. There's a need in Thailand for such long-term planning: to coordinate ministries and to handle questions of citizenship, taxation and education.

"To put matters into perspective, though, the 'brain gain' is really only a small, romantic part of the larger task of manpower development: to provide education and to upgrade skills so that Thailand can stay competitive into the next decade and beyond."

It Could Go Twelve Ways

The Cross-cultural Trainers

In a meeting room at the Arnoma Swissotel are nine expatriate managers representing Citibank, Esso Standard Thai, 3M Thailand, Hewlett-Packard, and the Regent and Grand Hyatt Erawan hotels. They are German, American, Italian, Australian and Indian. All have been in Thailand for only a few weeks, and they are here to learn about the Thai way of doing business. Their teacher is American consultant, Christopher Atkinson.

At a meeting room next door are gathered nine Thai managers from the same companies. Teaching them how to communicate with Westerners is Dr. Viboonpong Poonprasit, Thammasat University political science professor, and member of Chulalongkorn University's American Studies Program.

The 18 Thai and foreign executives are on the second of a three-day training course run by Cross-Cultural Management Co. Ltd. Pioneered over two decades ago by a Thai-American couple—Henry and Suchada Holmes—the course has so far been taught to 52 nationalities working in Thailand from a long roll call of major corporations: Unocal, Total, Caltex, Esso, Nestle, Seagate, Coca-Cola, Nike, Sony, Phillips, KLM and the World Bank.

The topic of this morning's first meeting is: "Understanding the Thai and Expatriate Systems."

Atkinson asks his nine expat managers to characterize their Thai co-workers. He chalks up their replies: "polite," "nice," "materialistic," "the *mai pen rai* attitude," "status conscious," "two-faced," and "lacking initiative."

Esso's Dorothy Williams clarifies the last phrase. "It's not that the Thais lack ambition or are afraid of work, but they tend to be followers rather than leaders."

"They're reluctant to make individual decisions," adds a hotel manager. "They prefer collective ones."

On the basis of these comments, Atkinson offers up a list of underlying core values related to national characteristics and the psychology of being Thai.

"First is pride and dignity," he explains to the group. "You could call it 'face' or 'honor.' People will leave a job if they are offended. A second value is personal loyalty. This is a relationship-based society. If one person leaves a job, others will follow. In this context, conflict avoidance is all important.

In meetings, people will hold back and wait to see what their superiors have to say. Communication is very much from the top down. Rank consciousness permeates Thai society. Strangers will ask you where you are from, how old you are, what your work is, and even how much money you make. They're not being rude. They're just looking to determine your social rank."

Atkinson then turns to a half dozen key Thai concepts. The Thai expression *krieng jai* has many possible definitions, but the one he offers is, "Taking extreme measures not to cause discomfort to another person's ego or emotions." At best, *krieng jai* entails a measure of tact; at worst, a refusal to disclose painful information. *Krieng jai* can impose a handicap in a multinational company where information is at a premium.

Other Thai values, however, simply ensure that relations are harmonious: *nam jai* (generosity with no expectation of reward), *jai yen* (self-control over emotions), *hai kiat* (giving respect), *alum-alui* (responding to extenuating circumstances) and *gan eng* (creating a comfortable social environment).

"If you can create an office atmosphere of *gan eng*," Atkinson observes, "you can crank up the work pressure as high as you want—as long as your employees know it's going to come down some time. You want to avoid a pressure-cooker office."

Mid-morning, the expat group breaks for coffee and then joins their Thai counterparts for a second session: "Solving Cross-Cultural Work Problems."

Dr. Viboonpong has already led the Thai contingent through elements of Western management style: assertiveness, accountability, results-orientation, and minimalizing gaps in rank to promote communication upward. He throws the differences in management styles out to general discussion. "For example, Thais are sensitive to direct criticism," he remarks. "In a company meeting, junior employees tend to stay silent out of fear of ridicule."

"It's true that people will lack confidence," agrees a Thai credit manager. "I won't speak up at a meeting unless I'm certain of what I want to say. And if I hear another idea from someone else, mine has to be better before I dare to speak."

"There are two problems here," observes Dr. Viboonpong. "One is language. You have to process English into Thai and back again, and by that time, the point of discussion might have passed. There is also a reluctance to interrupt—which is considered *very* impolite—especially if it's a superior who's talking. A Thai will wait for a senior to speak first, and then will not disagree. This goes back to the educational system, where you wait for the teacher to tell you what is right. In a company meeting with non-Thais, what strikes a Thai as conflict, actually is not. It's an interchange to reach a consensus. If you don't express your opinion, an expat will believe you haven't been thinking."

"A Westerner is looking for results," volunteers an American oil executive. "The results might build team spirit, which is good, but this is a by-product of the process."

"You have to get *tough*," adds Dorothy Williams in a strong New York accent. "Express your ideas. If other people don't like it, so what? I can't promote you if I don't know what you're thinking. So what if your boss is a jerk—you move forward."

This leads Dr. Viboonpong into a discussion of the Thai penchant for indirect communication. "It's difficult for foreigners to read the signs; to learn the indirect ways we have. A Thai smile can mean twelve things."

"Oh no!" Dorothy wails in despair. "Like the tones!"

The group breaks up laughing.

Dr. Viboonpong goes on to explain that a Thai smile can mean "Yes," "No," "I'm embarrassed," or "You're embarrassing me."

He gives the example of a traffic accident on Sukhumvit Road. The German driver emerges from his car with a furious scowl on his face. The Thai is smiling, meaning, "This is nothing to get upset about. We can handle this together." The smile only further infuriates the German, who's thinking, "*What's so funny?*"

The American oil executive poses a question. "Is it rude to ask a Thai person, 'Which smile are you using?'"

This prompts another round of laughter.

Dr. Viboonpong concludes with two observations on body language and eye contact. As a sign of respect, a Thai demands more body space when talking. Dr. Viboonpong does a comic turn, backing away from an imaginary conversational partner. "It's not that I think he has bad breath, but I just don't feel comfortable standing so close to him.

"The Thai also avoid touching other people. That's a serious gesture. And they avoid eye contact, especially with a superior. It's a polite way of paying respect. Eye contact is challenging. It can even be the prelude to a fight. In the West, eye contact is seen as a sign of honesty. Avoiding eye contact is shifty. In such indirect communication, it's easy for a Thai and non-Thai to mistake the signs they are exchanging."

The group breaks for lunch at noon. "The lights went on for me this morning," remarks George Romanyk, a new assistant manager at the Regent. "I wish I'd done this course eight weeks ago. I could've avoided some mistakes."

Adds construction engineer, Ian Redfern "My company has to downsize our expatriate staff and train Thai engineers to take their place. So this kind of training is essential."

In the afternoon, the Thais and expatriates break into small groups to work their way together through specific cross-cultural work problems. The next morning, the Thais will focus on understanding Western assertiveness and account-ability; the expatriates on Thai moral codes. In the afternoon, they'll work again in small groups to role-play key management concepts.

With the huge growth of multinational companies in Thailand, Cross-Cultural Management has expanded to fill the need for staff training.

"In the beginning, our training program was the Hank and Suchada Show," recalls founder, Dr. Henry Holmes, of his working partnership with his Thai wife. "Those were the days when Unocal, for example, was moving from a 30% expat workforce on its offshore rigs to less than 2%. We've hired additional trainers—some with a specialized focus on, say, French or Japanese companies."

Roy Tomizawa, who teaches the Japanese course, says that while the Thais and the Japanese share some values, they differ in degree. "Both are hierarchical societies; both place emphasis on creating harmony. But there are other Japanese values like *ishin denshin* (high context commun-ication, a shorthand between intimates), which Thais might find hard to understand. There's *dohryoko*, which can be translated as 'effort or initiative or accountability'—the lack of which the Japanese fault the Thais for; and *kaizen*, which is 'continual improvement'—never being satisfied with normal success."

The cross-cultural course itself is constantly being revised and improved upon, as Thai society itself changes. "We've moved the course to less emphasis on cultural issues and more on management problems," says Christopher Atkinson. "This isn't just a Peace Corps-style training course—it's for businessmen with real headaches in the management world."

"Another change I'd note," adds Dr. Viboonpong, "is that since 1990, we've amended the course to give our Thai participants more opportunity to learn about Western business values. As Thai companies expand, more Thais are going abroad and dealing with international clients. They're also moving into higher management levels. In fact, they're often the bosses of expat advisers."

"Some say there's an evolving multinational culture," notes Dr. Holmes. "But a study of 52 national branches of IBM showed that there were significant differences in management styles from country to country. The communications gap between junior and senior managers was highest in India and France; lowest in Israel and the Scandinavian countries. Thailand fell into the former camp; the US into the latter. There'll always be a demand for our kind of service."

A Thailand You Never Knew

The Economic Historians

Over the past four years, Drs. Pasuk Phongpaichit and Chris Baker have published three books that illuminate Thai history from the early nineteenth century up until November 1997 and the rise of the current Chuan Leekpai government. They tell you where Thailand has come from and where it might be going.

Their first book, *Thailand, Economy and Politics,* is an epochal 415-page investigation into the shifting economic currents that propelled Thai politics and culture up to the past decade. They offer a richly-detailed yet fast-paced "people's history" of pioneer rice farmers, Chinese immigrants, generals, bureaucrats, bankers, agribusiness exporters, student radicals, rural insurgents, Mafia kingpins, money politicians, global industrialists, and technocrats. Earlier histories of Thailand concentrate so much on the monarchy that they read like the biblical "Book of Kings." This book will change forever the way you think about Thailand.

At the turn of the nineteenth century, Thailand was a vast forest populated by no more than a million people scattered in riverine and coastal settlements. Given the scarcity of manpower, wealth was based on how many indentured peasants and slaves a local noble could control for corvee labor. But a revolution began in the 1840s. A huge market had developed for rice to feed the labor force of the new colonial economies of Asia. Thai peasants slipped their feudal bonds and fled for the "rice frontier"—clearing forests and draining swamps outside of official control.

"This peasantry was in no way 'traditional,'" emphasize Drs. Pasuk and Baker. "It was totally new. The resulting

society had many features common to frontier cultures—a high degree of self-sufficiency, egalitarian social ethics, resistance to government intervention, traditions of mutual assistance, and great mobility."

Drs. Pasuk and Baker demonstrate that this independent peasant society played a major role in the transformation of the Chakri dynasty into a true central government. By freeing the peasantry from slavery and corvee labor, King Chulalongkorn harnessed the expanding rice trade revenue in his struggle for political power over rival noble families. "Chulalongkorn set out to create a powerful monarchy ruling over a society of independent peasants."

In a parallel development, Chinese immigrants rose to become the rice barons and tax farmers of the nineteenth century. The Chakri kings balanced their economic power by inviting European investment, and they curtailed Chinese political power by ruthlessly suppressing riots and revolts. Through education, the sons of Chinese immigrants were absorbed into the official bureaucracy; through intermarriage, they entered the nobility.

Economic forces led to the 1932 overthrow of the absolute monarchy as well. Drs. Pasuk and Baker document how King Vajiravudh squandered his father, Chulalongkorn's inheritance, and how King Prajadhiphok mismanaged the fiscal crisis of the Great Depression. Following the king's abdication, Prime Minister Pibul Songkram's faction of military nationalists had originally been hostile to Chinese-dominated private industry. Favoring state enterprises, their motto was, "A Thai economy for the Thai people." But after World War II, Chinese bankers and industrialists moved aggressively to fill the void left by the Europeans. By the 1950s, military politicians were sitting on dozens of corporate boards. "Many of the politicians gave up the idea of attempting to slay the monster of emerging capital," Drs.

Pasuk and Baker note. "Instead, they mounted the monster's back and directed its fire against their enemies."

During the same period, the last frontier—the Northeastern plateau—was being invaded by road builders, loggers and agribusiness. *Isaan* nostalgia for an Edenic past is well-founded. "In 1950, the uplands were still largely a forest tract, with isolated strips of settlement along the rivers and streams, and strings of small trading outposts along the few trade routes."

The postwar boom in cash crops—sugar cane, maize, cassava, pineapples, oilseeds, cotton—changed all that. Between 1950 and 1979, the rural population outside the central region expanded from 13.4 million to 31.8 million. Government officials took tight control of the villages, either co-opting or repressing local leaders. Within a generation, the agrarian frontier was closed. With it went a uniquely self-sufficient village culture.

During the 1960s in Bangkok, a new generation of Sino-Thai entrepreneurs were busy transforming themselves from importers to manufacturers. Drs. Pasuk and Baker summarize Thailand's new breed of industrialist: "For Sukree in textiles, CP in agribusiness, Thaworn in automobiles, and many others, the ingredients of success were similar: a background in trading; a joint-venture partner for access to capital and technology; a good relationship with Bangkok Bank for working funds and business networking; and a batch of well-rewarded generals for government contracts, monopolistic privileges, and assorted favors."

The 1970s were a brutal time for Thailand. The downfall of a corrupt military triumvirate, brought about by student demonstrators, led to two years of intense turbulence that ended in savage right-wing suppression, and a mushrooming communist insurgency. By 1983, however, the insurgency was a spent force. With parliamentary elections restored, General Prem Tinsulanond presided over eight years of political stability and economic expansion that would provide the springboard for Thailand's economic boom.

Thailand's Boom! is a companion volume to *Thailand, Economy and Politics.* At the urging of friends, the authors followed up with a history of the 1986-1996 boom. The bare statistics of the ten-year boom are staggering. Manufactured exports multiplied twelve times—four fifths of Thailand's total. Urban population and per capita income doubled. Between 1985 and 1990, foreign investment increased ten times—yet this was only one *eighth* of domestic investment, as thousands of Thai industrial firms expanded into new global markets. Drs. Pasuk and Baker address the question: How did the boom happen?

The human base for the boom were some thirty Sino-Thai business families, with interests in over 800 companies, and who intermarried and invested in each other's enterprises.

"These networks of business and family connections became dense and complex," the authors comment. "Journalists and academics sometimes attempted to plot them. The results looked like microchip circuit diagrams, and they seemed to go on forever."

These families faced a crisis in the late 1970s. For two decades, a government policy of agricultural exports and import substitution had worked well. But with a worldwide decline in agricultural prices, Thailand suddenly faced a serious balance of payments problem. Joined by technocrats and the World Bank, the family conglomerates put pressure on the government to switch to the aggressive manufacture-export strategy favored by Asia's 'Four Tigers.' For a decade, the government dithered, relying on new foreign exchange earnings generated by tourism and remittances from Middle Eastern workers.

"The big break came in late 1984," the authors report. "By clinging to its old agriculture-led strategy as agricultural growth slowed, Thailand eventually ran out of reserves and creditors.

By attempting to stabilize the economy through rigid deflation, the government eventually provoked a major business crisis." The technocrats bit the bullet and devalued the baht. Simultaneously, they cut red tape and reformed procedures to boost manufactured exports. This was a timely move.

"Over the next couple of years, the revaluation of the yen and other Asian currencies multiplied the impact of the baht devaluation. The 100 baht which had cost 1180 yen in 1982, was going for just 508 yen by 1988. Industries began to shift from Japan to Thailand. Domestic capital flooded into industrial projects."

The business-dominated cabinets of Chatichai and Anand pushed through more financial reforms. "More importantly, government now managed the currency to promote manufactured exports," the authors note. "As the dollar continued to slip down against the yen, the baht grew steadily cheaper for Japanese traders and investors. From 1988 to 1995, the cost of 100 baht fell from 508 to 388 yen."

Between 1993 and 1995, a new Japanese factory was opening every three days. Toyota and Honda opened the biggest car plants outside Japan. Taiwan, Hong Kong and Korea soon joined the rush.

In 1991, the American computer giant Seagate became the country's largest private employer. Computer-parts exports, negligible in 1985, grew to 90 billion baht. And yet the authors emphasize that, "Foreign inflows may have sparked the boom. Thai investments made it a big boom." Two thirds of all investment was domestic.

For many years, Thailand was the fastest-growing economy in the world. "In the mid-1980s, the advent of Thailand's boom took most people by surprise," the authors conclude. "A new surprise may be more of a shock: the next stage is more difficult. How to keep the boom going. How to make sure the boom brings a better life for many more people."

So, what do you do when you've written a popular and critically-acclaimed study of the Thai economy's ten go-go years—*Thailand's Boom!*—and then the country goes bust?

Oops.

Well, you turn around and write an update—*Thailand's Boom and Bust*. The third book is 100 pages fatter than the second, and Drs. Pasuk and Baker have written two new chapters on the economic bust and politics since 1992. They have also added new material throughout the book that focuses on constitutional reform, the Assembly of the Poor, the Eighth Plan, the illegal economy, country music, TV soap operas, labor relations, NGOs, forest politics, educational changes, and the debate on Thai identity. Above all, they address the question: What went wrong?

"From 1986 to 1992, Thailand's boom had been based on the growth of export industries, promoted by domestic entrepreneurs and direct investment from East Asia," the authors recall. "The growth was real. The results were so spectacular that the international merchant banks and portfolio investors wanted a slice of the action. From 1992, Thailand was induced to open up its financial market and welcome foreign inflows. The World Bank, the international finance houses, and the financial press—from *Fortune* to *The Economist*—touted Thailand and the rest of miraculous Asia as a lucky-dip for financial profits."

This second wave of investments was not much concerned with factories. "Most came as portfolio funds, merchant bank loans, and speculative stashes—forms of capital which would move in and out at the speed of an electronic transfer. Thailand's local financial industry gorged on the inflows."

The authors enumerate the excesses that followed. "Too much was borrowed short and lent long. Too much was squandered on condos for housing mosquitoes. Some was plunged into over-ambitious and over-protected schemes. Some was simply stolen, as the BBC (Bangkok Bank of

Commerce) case revealed. Some was sunk in asset pyramids built by the inflows themselves."

The financial carousel crashed with the baht in July 1997. "When the baht imploded, the bubble burst, capital fled, liquidity disappeared, asset value lurched downwards, and the financial industry caved in. While the benefits of the boom were unequally distributed, the impact of the bust was indiscriminate. From top conglomerates to the smallest family concern, businesses built up over one, two, three and four decades faced annihilation."

The authors are succinct in laying the blame. "The bust was not simply the fault of careless lending by international finance. Nor was it simply caused by the pirate instincts of Thai businessmen and politicians. Rather it resulted in the explosive chemistry of mixing the two."

So where is Thailand headed now?

"Thailand now makes the international headlines as the center of a crisis of regional and global significance," the authors conclude. "Like an overnight star, the country seems dazed by the experience, by the extent of change, and by its new international fame. Beyond boom and beyond bust, the challenge is not to get back on the old path of economic growth, but to create the political framework, concept of public service, development strategy, and social values which allow many people to participate, contribute, and benefit."

Backstage with the Authors

Dr. Pasuk Phongpaichit is Associate Professor at Chulalong-korn's Faculty of Economics. A Rangsit native, she was awarded a Columbo scholarship to attend Melbourne's Monash University, graduating with an MA in Economics in 1971. On a Chulalongkorn scholarship to Cambridge University, she received her Ph.D. in 1979. That same year, she married Dr. Chris Baker—author of four books on India—

who had taught Asian history, sociology and politics at Cambridge. Since 1979, Dr. Baker has worked in advertising and marketing in Bangkok.

Excerpts from an interview with the authors:

JE: How did you begin writing *Thailand, Economy and Politics*?

Dr. Baker: For six or seven years, I'd been after her to write something broad. We began the book after the May Events in 1992. She'd done a substantial bit of work already—

Dr. Pasuk: But the book became a *passion* after May '92. We wrote the book on weekends in a beach bungalow in Cha-am. We'd write, then argue, then rewrite.

Dr. Baker: People would see us walking on the beach, screaming at each other, and think we were getting a divorce.

Dr. Pasuk: But we talked things through. It was a learning experience because we come from such different backgrounds and disciplines. Male, female. Thai, *farang*. Chris's field is history, mine economics. His background is business, mine academic. Each had to convince the other. Our fights actually served to enhance the book.

Dr. Baker: *Thailand's Boom!* went a lot easier, because by this point we knew what we wanted to say.

JE: Turning to the substance of your first two books, what are your main points of argument?

Dr. Pasuk: Economics, in society, is not a mechanism. People are doing things in an environment. They are taking opportunities, as in the frontier rice economy. People make their own societies. This one country was created out of many different countries; by ordinary people, peasants. Previous histories have emphasized the monarchy. But the people have been the basis of the economy, and the king responded. Our focus is on economic development, the free peasantry, and the immigrant Chinese.

JE: Your chapters on the conflict between the city and the village—*muang* and *ban*—seem to take the side of the traditional villages in the face of development.

Dr. Baker: I don't mean to suggest some kind of peasant romanticism. On the frontier, there was often not enough to eat. There was disease and banditry.

JE: But when you talk about the "invasion" of the Northeast by the central government in the fifties and sixties—deforestation, roads, schools, cash crops, tractors, processing plants, banks—wasn't this just normal rural development? The kind that's happened all around the world? You make it sound sinister.

Dr. Pasuk: There was a momentum involved that brought access to technology, international markets, banking. The government's role was predatory, and deliberate. There was a communist threat. The farmers were encouraged to mono-crop—and after prices fall, what do they do? They're left without skills or labor, and there's no forest to fall back on. They have no cash for investment to start up other crops, plus their family labor has been dispersed to the city. The political environment of anti-communism led to environmental changes, and had an enormous cost to the social fabric. It was a deliberate breaking down of community unity.

JE: Provincial politicians—much like Lyndon Johnson—developed a rural patronage base before moving on to national power. What motivates provincial politicians in Thailand? Is it money or power?

Dr. Pasuk: You can't separate money and power. They go together. People make money, then reach for formal power. Kamnan Po [*jao por*, Mafia boss of Chonburi] boasts openly about his power, but it's informal. He doesn't have the education to be an MP, but his sons do—and are rising rapidly and receiving official honors. They are in this to control the decision making process. Before, provincial politicians had to share with the generals, but now elections enhance their power. Before, they had to defer to the *jao sua* [big businessmen] of Bangkok, but now they say, "We can run this by ourselves."

JE: You mention that *jao por* form a minority of politicians, though a colorful one.

Dr. Pasuk: Yes. In the last elections, there were many local lawyers, teachers and straight businessmen who were elected. But you can't avoid the fact that the big money is still being made by "primitive accumulation"—logging, drugs, smuggling, prostitution, gambling. This isn't in the book, but many honest politicians go astray once they're in parliament. There's party pressure. The system is built to co-opt them. But there is new blood coming up, post-1992. The countryside is changing fast too. People are emerging from the old system. With NGO help, they're focusing on the environment, women's issues, small farmer groups. Community leaders are becoming more articulate.

JE: What percentage of villages are really affected by NGOs?

Dr. Baker: It's not really a game of numbers. It's an idea network. Ideas in activity, in an economy in transition.

JE: Turning to the present economic crisis, did you see it coming?

Dr. Pasuk: We missed out, like everyone else, how stupid the money movers could be.

Dr. Baker: Those 24-year-olds in Hugo Boss suits.

Dr. Pasuk: The Thai overestimated themselves in being able to handle huge inflows of money. Policy makers followed the lead of Britain and the US in opening markets. They didn't realize the danger to a small, weak economy. When I asked one prominent Thai policy maker if we had an independent economic policy, he replied, "No, we follow the big guys."

JE: This is May 1999. Where does Thailand stand now?

Dr. Pasuk: I have a hunch that the recovery will happen quickly. Once confidence returns, and the process of rethinking in the banking sector, production will pick up fast. But the growth won't be the same as the previous 10-15-year period.

JE: Will the economy be structured differently?

Dr. Baker: For twenty years—1955 to 1975—Thailand looked to the US for economic development. For the next twenty, it looked to Japan. After the crash, Thailand turned back to the US, and made it easy for Western firms to get in. But they're not coming back, except as asset strippers. What is happening is that the Japanese are quietly buying out their joint venture partners in manufacturing. And you have the Miyazawa Plan of a year ago: 1.54 billion dollars worth of loans.(Finance Minister) Tarrin was quick to grab it.

Dr. Pasuk: Southeast Asia is Japan's industrial backyard. They can't let it rot. The adjustment that's going on is interesting, not just for economic growth, but for social services—putting our house in order. That we're not going to grow so fast is maybe a good thing.

JE: Chuan Leekpai has been in power for a year and nine months. How do you rate his administration?

Dr. Pasuk: A six out of ten.

Dr. Baker: I agree.

Dr. Pasuk: We lost time in believing the IMF package—based on Latin American bailouts. We thought that all we had to do was boost investor confidence to save Thailand. A more independent policy began to form a year ago, and has accelerated in the last six months. That's where the six comes from.

Dr. Baker: The IMF has changed too. They're asking Thailand to enlarge their government deficit. Pure heresy!

JE: What about Chuan's social policies?

Dr. Baker: It's unfair to criticize people while they're in a crisis and struggling to get the IMF off their backs. But in general, the experience has demystified policy makers as the economy fell in a heap. That minds have changed had political consequences.

Dr. Pasuk: If the upturn comes too quickly, the learning process will be lost. This crisis produced a steep learning curve: a rethinking of the urban-rural balance in policy making.

JE: Is there a benefit to the crisis?

Dr. Pasuk: Definitely. If there was no crisis, no constitution would have been passed. Everyone was against it: the military, the bureaucracy, the business elite, judges, big people in politics. Restructuring politics will make for more relevant economic policy making.

JE: There is a "golden land" (*suwanaphum*) vision of Thailand becoming a center for the prosperity of its Southeast Asian neighbors. Do you see that happening?

Dr. Pasuk: I don't really see that in Indochina or Burma. Thai businessmen are neither liked nor trusted. But the big market will be China. We're making the right moves there. That will be the important outlet for the future.

Epilogue

I hadn't seen Doctor Penguin in years when I ran into him at the Danish ambassador's house on March 4, 1999. His hair was longer, he was older and fatter, but his chuckle was still irrepressibly evil. He had been based in Singapore for the past three years, doing post-production work on a 13-part TV series called "Dr. Penguin's Magical World."

"Singapore? *You*?" I asked incredulously. "Don't they keep records down there?"

"They sure do. When I got to immigration at Changi Airport, they said, 'Now you're going to be a good boy, aren't you?' I promised I would."

The Doc was walking with a limp, courtesy of a broken ankle he'd acquired after falling off a horse in Hungary— one of the stops on his "Magical World" tour that took him to Thailand, Malaysia, Singapore, Borneo, Cambodia, the Maldives, Pakistan, Hong Kong, Australia, Bali and Burma.

"In Burma, the cops wanted to confiscate my film at the airport," he told me. "So I did a sleight-of-hand trick and they wound up with empty canisters. That was one time when being a magician came in handy."

"Dr. Penguin's Magical World" premiered to rave reviews at the MIP documentary convention in Cannes. The series will be broadcast in the United States on the Public Broadcasting System; in the United Kingdom on BBC; and in Australia on the Discovery Channel. Other deals are pending, and the magician may finally see some money.

Dr. Penguin invited me down for two shows of his Magic Circus at the Singapore Zoo. From Russia, Japan, Australia, Holland, the Philippines, Sweden, Hong Kong and the USA came magicians, musicians, mime artists, belly dancers, acrobats, chainsaw jugglers, tightrope walkers and freeloading journalists. I was flown down to Singapore on SAS business class and put up at the Sheraton Tower on Scotts Road. I gorged. I swilled. I laughed my butt off.

Through the rest of 1999, Dr. Penguin's Magic Circus will travel to Nepal, Thailand, Laos, Cambodia, Vietnam and Singapore. For a New Year's finale, Dr. Penguin is rounding up forty artists for a Millennium Bash in Bali.

"2000 is our year!" crowed the Doc in his last e-mail to me. "This should be the first tour of its kind since the seventies, when I took the Magic Circus through Afghanistan, India, Sri Lanka, Nepal, etc. That time we were a road show, now you can say we're a flying circus!"

Orathai Karnchanachusak temporarily quit politics after losing her parliamentary seat when the Palang Dhama party collapsed in the 1996 elections. She married her boyfriend, Nitapan Tanajaro, son of the former Thai Army commander. With the extinction of Palang Dhama, she is casting about for another party to join, but for now she is content in taking care of Om, her four-month-old son.

Sara-Jane Angsuvarnsiri moved her restaurant from Langsuan to the ground floor of the Sindhorn Tower on Wireless Road. The 220-seat restaurant is bright, airy, tall-ceilinged, and decorated with exuberantly-colorful Thai paintings. I found Sara Jane manning the cash register. She looked great.

"We moved two years ago," she told me. "The Langsuan building was old, and parking was impossible. So I decided to move to the Sindhorn Tower to bring Isaan cooking into the twenty-first century."

The new Sara Jane's Restaurant serves both *Isaan* and Italian food. Her prices are still low, and at lunch-time, every table is packed.

"My family's doing good," Sara Jane reports. "Joy, the eldest, is in her third year at Chulalongkorn, and Meri's at

Bangkok University. Both are studying mass communications."

MR Supinda Chakraband's latest project was to have the new production of *The King and I* filmed in Thailand. She failed.

The Triumph showroom of Boonprasom Sirivongse and Roy Barrett is thriving—in the midst of the economic doldrums.

"Right now, Boonprasom is leading a group of 15 European tourists on a Triumph motorcycle tour of South Thailand," Roy reports.

"Last I heard, they were in Phuket. Then they'll go on to Songkhla, Surat Thani and Koh Samui. Greg Hondow is no longer working for us. He married a Thai girl and opened a restaurant in the neighborhood here called *Pooying Pom Yao*— The Long-haired Girl."

Nanthida Kaewbuasai married the son of a political kingpin; she has a four-year-old daughter nicknamed Plaeng (Song); and she goes from triumph to triumph in concerts and albums. My palms broke out in a sweat when I phoned her.

Raymond Eaton is still happily single and living in his spectacular house. The devaluation of the baht hit his Intregra Group by raising the cost of imported materials, but buoyed it too, by making the price of his exports more competitive.

His major sales product now is the "Turbolog"—an on-board computer for trucks that monitors speed, fuel consumption, and the driver's performance. Since the Asian financial crisis, the big trucking, oil, and cement companies have become more cost conscious—and willing to invest in Eaton's Turbolog.

Bernard Trink is still cranking out "The Nite Owl."

General Kitti Ranachaya is still playing golf and is also running the New Aspiration Party's election campaign in upper South Thailand.

Khanitha Akranitikul had to close her Chiang Mai silk factory, but her showroom on Suriwong is still going strong. She has since opened a second showroom at Oriental Place.

Henry Holmes and Cross-Cultural Management have weathered the Asian crisis well. Even companies that have downsized continue to send employees to the cross-cultural course. "This serves to boost morale," Dr. Holmes comments. "Because if a company is planning to lay you off, it's not going to make the investment to send you on a training course." His courses have also expanded to help Thai executives to move into the place of expat managers—a trend that will only accelerate in future, as companies look to cut costs.

After *Thailand's Boom and Bust*, Dr. Pasuk Phongpaichi published *Guns, Girls, Gambling, Ganja: Thailand's Illegal Economy and Public Policy*. Together with co-authors Sungsidh Piriyarangsan and Nualnoi Treerat, she explored Thailand's thriving corruption industry. Previously, she had written *Thailand: Corruption and Democracy* with Mr. Sungsidh. She is now at work on a book about gambling in Las Vegas, Australia, Great Britain, Malaysia and Thailand. She is also writing a study of social movements in Thailand: farmers, fishermen, hill tribes, slum dwellers, female industrial workers.

Dr. Chris Baker was well qualified to write *Thailand's Boom and Bust.* After the crisis, he lost his marketing job at Riche Monde. He is collaborating with Dr. Pasuk on a general introduction to modern Thailand for the non-academic reader, and a biography of Pridi Banomyong. He is also writing a long-term history of Thailand for Cambridge University Press. "Pasuk will make some contribution, but I'll get top billing," he says with a smile.

About the Author

James Eckardt, a noble New Yorker, stepped ashore in Songkhla 23 years ago, married, sired four children, and ascended to Bangkok in 1992 to become associate editor of *Manager Magazine*. With the demise of *Manager* in July 1997, he worked as editor of the *Phuket Gazette* until February 1998, when he moved to Cambodia to cover the national elections for the *Phnom Penh Post*. After eight months in Cambodia, he returned to Bangkok to become editor-at-large for Scand-Media—the Viking correspondent in Thailand.

Bangkok People is his fifth book. He has also written the novels *Boat People* and *Running with the Sharks,* and the story collections *Waylaid by the Bimbos* and *On the Bus with Yobs, Frogs, Sods and the Lovely Lena*. He is working on a sixth book, mostly about Cambodia.